Praise for Mary Hayes Grieco's
The NEW KITCHEN MYSTIC

"If you've never read Mary Hayes Grieco before, you're in for such a treat. I almost envy you. This is delicious wisdom and the finest quality writing. Mary is optimistic and passionate about the struggles, silliness, and successes we all experience on the path of everyday enlightenment."

Rosanne Bane, author of *Around the Writer's Block*

"In *The New Kitchen Mystic*, Mary Hayes Grieco has crafted a companion book that's as endearing as it is enlightening. With her unique blend of storytelling and philosophical insight, Mary coaxes us to revisit our perceptions and the way we live, thus enabling us to shape the adventures that await."

**Mike Dooley, *New York Times* bestselling author of
Infinite Possibilities and *Leveraging the Universe***

"I *love* Mary's inspirational book! It's perfect. Beautiful. Elegant. Useful. It is a wonderful holiday gift."

Andrew Ramer, author of *Ask Your Angels*

"These little essays share laughter, wonder, self-examination, growth, and loss—everything that goes into the sensational stew called living. Love it!"

Minneapolis Star Tribune

the NEW
KITCHEN
MYSTIC

A COMPANION FOR SPIRITUAL EXPLORERS

Mary Hayes Grieco

ATRIA PAPERBACK
New York London Toronto Sydney New Delhi

BEYOND WORDS
Hillsboro, Oregon

ATRIA PAPERBACK
A Division of Simon & Schuster, Inc.
1230 Avenue of the Americas
New York, NY 10020

BEYOND WORDS
20827 N.W. Cornell Road, Suite 500
Hillsboro, Oregon 97124-9808
503-531-8700 / 503-531-8773 fax
www.beyondword.com

Copyright © 1992, 2008, 2013 by Mary Hayes Grieco
Originally published under the title *The Kitchen Mystic* by Hazelden Foundation, 1992, and under the title *Be a Light* by Waterwheel Publishing, 2008.

Managing editor: Lindsay S. Brown
Editor: Emily Han
Copyeditor: Claire Foster
Proofreader: Linda Meyer
Design: Devon Smith
Composition: William H. Brunson Typography Services

First Atria Paperback/Beyond Words trade paperback edition June 2013

ATRIA PAPERBACK and colophon are trademarks of Simon & Schuster, Inc. Beyond Words Publishing is an imprint of Simon & Schuster, Inc. and the Beyond Words logo is a registered trademark of Beyond Words Publishing, Inc.

For more information about special discounts for bulk purchases, please contact Simon & Schuster Special Sales at 1-866-506-1949 or business@simonandschuster.com.

The Simon & Schuster Speakers Bureau can bring authors to your live event. For more information or to book an event, contact the Simon & Schuster Speakers Bureau at 1-866-248-3049 or visit our website at www.simonspeakers.com.

Manufactured in the United States of America

10 9 8 7 6 5 4 3 2 1

Library of Congress Cataloging-in-Publication Data

Hayes Grieco, Mary.
    The new kitchen mystic : a companion for spiritual explorers / Mary Hayes Grieco. — Atria pbk./Beyond Words trade pbk. ed.
        pages   cm
    1. Self-actualization (Psychology).   2. Spiritual life.   I. Title.
    BF637.S4.H394   2013
    204'.4—dc23

                                                    2012047983

ISBN 978-1-58270-426-5
ISBN 978-1-4767-1473-8 (eBook)

The corporate mission of Beyond Words Publishing, Inc.: *Inspire to Integrity*

To my husband, Fred, one of my teachers

CONTENTS

Contents

INTRODUCTION

There are no strangers—only friends we haven't met yet.
Irish proverb

Hello, my friend. I imagine that you, like me, are someone who wishes to shed your fears and limitations, groom your best self into being, and shine like the sun—illumined from within by your soul and its loving purposes. But the path of self-mastery and the quest for spiritual liberation is by nature a challenging one—a hero's journey—and it requires the presence of dedicated traveling companions and frequent doses of inspiration and encouragement. Throughout the years, my path has been lit by the daily presence of an inspiring book—a book that, like a friend, reflects me to myself like a mirror, and keeps me company. I have always treasured certain books, the ones written by people who engaged life fully, and who were able to distill their personal experience into words that shine with the universal, golden nobility of something we call *truth*.

In high school, I was a lonely philosopher and an oddball who was warmly befriended by Henry David Thoreau and Kahlil Gibran. I traipsed through the crowded halls with a battered copy of *Walden Pond* or *The Prophet* in my purse, and I retreated to a private space at least once a day to seek solace in reading and to find myself again. When I traveled around America in my early twenties, Walt Whitman's *Song of Myself* lived in my backpack and spoke with me at bedtime, wherever that turned out to be. When I was in my thirties and forties, I found comfort and guidance in several different translations of the Bhagavad Gita. Now I'm in my fifties, and as I sit in my favorite chair, writing this, I have a copy of *The Power of Now* nearby that is starting to show signs of much use.

Life is glorious, but it is difficult, and we need all the support that we can get. For many of us, it has been a path riddled with obstacles, disappointments, unexpected losses, and even some trauma. The landscape of our existence plays out externally and internally. Even if we have the good fortune to enjoy a gracious and fulfilling outer life, we can still feel vexed by internal struggle as we attempt to address some shortcoming or excess in our character.

My personal struggles have been both external and internal. I've had to cope with a certain amount of difficulty throughout my life, and I've also had to master my high-maintenance personality—an extra-sensitive temperament that gets mired in insecurity and derailed by intense emotions or leftover ghosts from the past. I've done my best to make good use of my sensitivity, and gain what wisdom I can from my pain. I've discovered that, once integrated, my life experience allows me to serve as a potent catalyst for the growth of others. I have found a measure of peace with the hard work that goes into mastering the difficult facets of my existence: self-mastery leads to human greatness, and that's what interests me most of all.

I have looked greatness in the eye a few times—I have been blessed in this life by several great souls, my spiritual teachers. In the presence of these masterful people, I witnessed a loving, universal state of consciousness and a steady way of serving the world from the heart of that consciousness. I became inspired to find my own greatness—to become the best me that I can be. I am determined to discover my purpose, find the best way I can serve the world, and make a positive difference. I can't settle for less than that. It is a flame in my heart.

This passion was first kindled for me when I was a girl reading *The Lives of the Saints*, sheltered by the shadows of the staircase in my family's home. It was a home that was filled with tender love and terrible alcoholic chaos. When I grew up, that little flame of vision was fanned into a blaze as I stood in awe at a fire ceremony conducted by Brahman priests at the home of my meditation teacher in India. The ceremony was dedicated to ending the ills of society; I went home changed, freshly committed to that goal. Later, my restless passion for illumination and world service was recognized, contained, and guided by my mentor Dr. Edith Stauffer. With loving dispassion, she showed me how to heal my wounds. She charged me to carry her life work—teaching forgiveness—out into the world. It became my life work, too, and I plan on teaching as many people as I can how to forgive. I hope you will read my work *Unconditional Forgiveness: A Simple and Proven Method to Forgive Everyone and Everything* and find new freedom and purpose by healing your life story with forgiveness.

The fire inside me became steady and sealed into my cells with the firm touch of my wise teacher's aged hand upon mine. Now it glows in the votive candle on the altar next to my chair when I meditate every morning. It simmers on the stove as I make dinner for my family. It informs the workshops that I teach. It heals the pain of others. It has brought me into my true self, and sent me out into the world, far and wide.

Along the way, I wrote this collection of essays, though I did not have a conscious intention of writing a book. When I wrote some of these pieces, I was merely driven by the necessity of writing myself out of darkness into clarity and peace of mind. I wrote other pieces because I was in a full-to-bursting state of gratitude and insight, dying to share my thoughts and experiences with other spiritual explorers. It was a pleasant surprise to me that my writing was helpful to others. In what seemed like a happy accident, my essays were discovered and published as a collection by Hazelden in 1992. *The Kitchen Mystic: Spiritual Lessons Hidden in Everyday Life* was a small daily inspiration book, of the kind that Hazelden was known for in those days. It turned out to be a book that wouldn't go away—a friend of mine calls it "the little book that could." Long after it went out of print, people kept it, remembered it, and contacted me hoping to buy copies for Christmas, birthdays, and Mother's Day. It seems like no one who stumbled across it ever bought fewer than four copies.

Over these last twenty years I have been blessed to meet many people who loved *The Kitchen Mystic*. These friendly fans like to show me their copy of my book: dog-eared, streaked with yellow highlighter, and with their own enthusiastic notes scribbled in the margins. These strangers touch my arm and look at me knowingly as they quote me to myself, as if we are old friends, meeting again. They lean close to my face and tell me earnestly how loyal they feel to my little book, and how faithfully it's been there for them. *I keep it by my bedside . . . I always take it with me on vacation . . . it's on the kitchen counter where I can see it . . . here it is, right here in my purse, like always! I love this book—such fresh thinking!* Looking at those worn, tattered copies of *The Kitchen Mystic*, I am reminded of my relationship with those few special books in my life, and with a thrill of understanding, I see that my book is their *friend*. It is a favorite book with timeless ideas, a trusted companion on the bumpy road to spiritual fulfillment. It is *perennial*, as they call it in the publishing world. I am honored and glad that the good people at Beyond Words/Atria Books have "discovered" this book of mine, and that it will enjoy a rebirth as *The New Kitchen Mystic*—ready to meet old friends and new ones.

So, friend, I pray that this book will be a good companion to you on your daily way. Together we will walk in the inspiring company of great people who have gone before us. Each of the well-loved masters, mystics, and social heroes of the past have held their illumined hearts out to the world like a lamp in the darkness. So can we. Thank God we are not alone, you and I. We are together, your heart and mine, in the Great Heart that beats in the center of Creation for all of us.

Mary Hayes Grieco
Autumn 2012

A CREATION STORY

And God saw that it was good.
Book of Genesis

In the beginning, there was nothing. It was The Void, the only inhabitant of cold eternity. Then there was a spark! An impulse for something. It sprang into being, and tumbled and ricocheted around, multiplying itself a thousandfold in an instant. The sparks became a sound, a vast breathing sound, inhaling and exhaling in the darkness. The sound became Light, an infinite field of light. Without birth, without death, it always was.

The Light awakened to its own Self. It was the Great Self, a vast field of light illuminated from within by love. The primordial sound sang endlessly in its heart. *I wish to create!* Spirit said, and it breathed out a Universe in an instant with a *Bang!* Galaxies and worlds spun into being in a great dance. There were worlds and worlds—some cold, some molten, some with delicate little veils of atmosphere. One of the worlds was Gaia, blue-green and virginal. *You are special to me*, Spirit thought. *I will mate with you. I will impregnate you with my essence. You will bear me a child, in a form that reflects my own nature.*

Gaia conceived. The single cell in the womb of her oceans multiplied and grew, like a tadpole, like a frog, like a dinosaur, like a bird, like a mammal. It roared like a lion, climbed like an ape, and sang like a whale. It diversified and improvised, and the web of life was woven with intricacy, with texture and color, with lively and impeccable balance.

When the moment was right, the human beings emerged. In the heart of the human beings was the sound of God. In their breath was the tiny essence of the Great Spirit, the great breath. In the brain of the humans was a dormant center of light, awaiting the moment of kindling. In their nervous systems was the complex communications network between Spirit and form, the pathway of light into matter. In the DNA of the human beings is the plan for God to wake up and know Himself, to express Herself, to live a loving, dynamic life in material form. Inside my own self God is waking up, stretching painfully through the slow rocky density of matter . . . clumsily transcending the emotional heritage of my ancient defensive systems to remember the peace of my essence.

There is a divine spark . . . of that great Light embodied as a soul in the small self of every human being. We see the light of the soul expressed as a certain spiritual quality in the personality: love, kindness, generosity, will, joy, patience. The Great Spirit looks sleepily out of my eyes, out of your eyes, in ever increasing numbers of people around the world—reaching within and spreading without to share the awareness that God dwells within me, as me. God dwells within you, as you. We are the children of God in the lap of the Earth. We are the Light. Let us create!

THE KITCHEN MYSTIC

Sultan, saint, pickpocket—love has everyone by the ear,
dragging us to God by secret ways.
I never knew that God, too, desires us.

Rumi

I'd like to suggest a new name for the spirituality that is spreading like a quiet fire through our society. I see it in myself and seekers around me who pass through, incorporating the gifts of different paths. It's a synthesis of wisdom from both the East and West, a mix of Judeo-Christian principles, yoga, Buddhism, Twelve Step philosophy, Earth religions, and a personal medley of experience and growth. I call it Kitchen Mysticism.

The kitchen is where you perform important but mundane acts like cooking, eating, washing dishes, and confiding with your close friends. Kitchen Mysticism cultivates the awareness of direct, intimate communion with the Divine in the arena of everyday existence. It's a very personal path, and there are as many ways of walking it as there are people.

Kitchen Mystics may or may not attend an organized church. They find convenient places to commune and worship: the shower, the car, a park bench at sunset. You will often spot Mystics muttering earnestly to someone no one else can see, or stopping mid-project with an entranced look—listening. They are performing one of the major practices of faith: conducting an ongoing, loving dialogue between the God Within and the God Without.

Kitchen Mystics have rich internal lives and so have smaller appetites for external stimulation than other people. We pay for entertainment less often because we see that truth is stranger than fiction anyway. Passionate spiritual seekers, we find ourselves involved in a never-ending mystery story that unfolds with subtlety, finesse, and occasional high drama. There is a benevolent plot afoot, and its conspirators are everywhere—seen and unseen. Their mission: the end of our fears and limitations, resulting in our spiritual awakening! It's harrowing, uplifting, and more thrilling than *Star Trek* because we ourselves are the main characters! We Kitchen Mystics entertain each other with accounts of synchronicity and the breakthrough insights we experience.

Mystics find meaning in many places. The Divine is always hiding clues and love letters for us in daily life, and it's fun to discover these. It's like an Easter egg hunt: I wink and nod at my friend when I find another colored egg. Then we laugh together at the humor and cleverness that hid the treasure in plain sight. If I am struggling to uncover new understanding, I hear a voice whispering to me. "Warm . . . warmer . . . cooler . . . warmer . . . HOT!" I will eventually find it, or something will take me gently by the hand and show me before I feel too dejected.

Almost every Kitchen Mystic has a special object of contemplation and worship, something from the physical world that says "God" directly to you—and maybe no one else. My daughter sees the Divine in a common rock. When she was tiny and I was trying to hustle her off to daycare, she would stop several times to pick up stones and talk to them. Then she'd put them in her pockets. Now when we return from traveling, her suitcase inevitably rattles with new friends, stones that have called out to her. She won't let me dispose of them—they're sacred. White ones are extra special. She can spot a chip of white quartz in a bag of fishtank gravel and insist that I meditate on it with her. I don't get God in rocks, but I think it is important for Mystics to support each other's contemplations.

I see God in onions. I always have. I remember when I first saw my mother slicing into an onion; I was about six. I stopped my playing, awestruck. What was this vegetable that was so pure, so watery-white? It was many-layered, its concentric rings like a mandala, making mounds of perfect circles as they fell open onto the cutting board . . . *wow*. I begged her to let me cut some, despite her warning that it would make my eyes burn. I can remember concentration and reverence welling up within me as I awkwardly tried to make perfect slices. My eyes *did* burn. I had to stop after a few cuts, but I vowed that I would understand onions some day and cook with them myself.

Later that summer my Dad took us all out for a rare visit to a fast-food joint—a real treat. My younger brothers and sisters ordered hamburgers with ketchup, but my Dad turned to me and said, "How about it, honey—you want everything on it?"

"*Everything on it.*" Those words struck me like a sacred gong, a mantra given to me personally that would guide me all of my days. I nodded mutely, not even understanding what these words mean in your usual hamburger joint—I only knew that this was a spiritual risk I was destined to take. When my hamburger arrived, I peeked under the soggy bun and was thrilled to see the chopped grilled onions sprinkled like tiny translucent pearls amid the steaming ketchup, mustard, and pickles. I ate my burger in a blissful trance, convinced that I would eat them "with everything on it" forevermore.

My contemplation of the Mystery in the onion continues to this day. As an artist I have paid homage to my friend the onion by creating a stained glass window of an underground bulb; it hangs in a local food co-op. As a cook, I have learned how to coax the sweetness out of an onion, and to tame its fire into mellow good humor. I can cut them now without crying, but not without pausing for a brief moment. Red onions are especially divine. I hold a slice up to the sunlight pouring in through the kitchen window, and it glows like a fine piece of antique glass. Cool and watery-white with layers delicately edged in imperial purple—strong, humble, peaceful—and a fiery nub of spring green in the center, aspiring to sprout. "Ah! Look at *this* one!" I cry to my husband and daughter nearby. They look at each other and smile at me tolerantly. "That's a really nice one." They don't see God in onions the way I do, but they know that we Mystics have to stick together.

 Listen to Mary tell you about her love of onions in an audio reading of the story "The Kitchen Mystic."

SPIRITUALITY
AND RELIGION

I believe deeply that we must find, all of us together, a new spirituality.
This new concept ought to be elaborated alongside the religions in
such a way that people of goodwill could adhere to it.

His Holiness the 14th Dalai Lama

"Don't throw the baby out with the bath-water," the old saying goes. In recent years I have heard former churchgoers say, "I'm a recovering Catholic," as if referring to a dangerous disease. Some traditional churches give their congregations dire warnings about any kind of spiritual exploration not strictly based in the Christian Bible. They view other paths as scattered, shallow, or worse, direct conspiracy with the devil! I feel frustrated and sad when I hear this polarization between tradition and a personal, open-ended spiritual search. There is a need for both of these things. In my life, it's time to bring spirituality and religion together.

What's the distinction between spirituality and religion? Many people don't believe there is one. Yet all of us have known loving, gentle souls who never entered a church in their lives, as well as unkind people who went to church every Sunday. Religions, in and of themselves, don't necessarily produce spiritual people, and people can grow and have spiritual lives whether they follow a religion or not.

My definition of spirituality is: *the cultivated awareness that I am an individual expression of an immortal Being whose nature is love, peace, and creativity.* Let's take this apart to understand it better.

Awareness means being cognizant, conscious, and knowing in a responsive way. It is a state of being and perception rather than a collection of beliefs. You develop it with education and training, helpful techniques, life experiences, and ongoing attention. *Cultivated awareness* is a state of awareness you deliberately grow, like a gardener.

An individual expression of an immortal Being means that I am a small but important part of something much greater than me. Something was here before I became who I am now, and it will exist after I lay this body down at my death. I am that something, that Being, expressing myself here in my brief time. This Being also expresses itself all around me as different people, creatures, and objects that make up the world. Like water in the ocean, we are defined as drops for a short time, but we are always part of the whole. The ocean exists before, during, and after the drops express themselves individually in the material world.

The nature of the Being is *love*, *peace*, and *creativity*. These are spiritual qualities that religions instilled in us for ages, as are faith, hope, joy, compassion, courage, kindness, universal brotherhood, and strength.

The challenge of our spiritual journey is to heal and clarify our individual personalities on all levels—physical, emotional, intellectual, and spiritual—so that we can experience these spiritual qualities, not just hope for them. Pierre Teilhard de Chardin expressed it best when he said that we think that we are human beings seeking a divine experience, but the key to our spiritual liberation is realizing that we are divine Beings having a human experience. We are Spirit, enjoying a risky sojourn as a higher mammal on planet Earth.

Our bodies and psyches are thick and dark with pain and ignorance, like a lamp with a blackened glass chimney. "We see as through a glass, darkly" (1 Corinthians 13:12). The spiritual journey is the cleaning and polishing of the glass so that the burning light within may radiate outward, illuminating itself and its environment. As we become enlightened, we embody more and more energy and happiness in our direct knowledge that we are an expression of God. Anything we do in our daily lives to cultivate this love, peace, and creativity is a spiritual practice.

Spirituality is a personal matter, and every one of us has a completely unique spiritual journey. Many people today are exploring spirituality with great independence and zeal. We flit from flower to flower like enthusiastic hummingbirds—a little yoga here, a little shamanism there, a chapter or two of inner-child work, six of the Twelve Steps. There's always something beckoning us to new levels of love, freedom, and power. Today, spiritual seekers have broken from distorted, shame-based religions and are reveling in a buffet of new ideas and expanding consciousness.

For me, that was fine and good for a number of years. It was exactly what I needed to do. But after a while, I was dissatisfied with traveling a little way on many different paths, and I began to think that perhaps religious monogamy wasn't such a bad idea. As in relationships, an open-ended situation can take you only so far. There is something extremely valuable for me now in committing to the parameters of a whole religion. It is the challenge and the gift of a deepening experience—diving below the sparkling surface and meeting the fears, the problems, the dark side, and the Mystery. I know in my heart that my spiritual journey will take me to new edges, new frontiers, and beyond to real fulfillment if I have the courage and discipline to stay on my special path. I am ready to unite my spirituality and my religion and settle down.

A religion can be our path of spiritual exploration. It can provide us with community, rituals, rules, limits, mythology, inspired writings, spiritual practices, and models of spiritual mastery. Every true religion has a wellspring of transforming spiritual energy. A living religion is whole and internally consistent. There is an overall balance and integrity to this path that brings depth and richness to seekers as they mature.

Many people take part in religious rituals because they are expected socially. Some people are ready to do more spiritual work, while others observe from a safe comfort zone. There's nothing wrong with the latter. Onlookers can glean spiritual benefits from observing a religious community. Everyone proceeds at his or her own pace.

Oftentimes the most enthusiastic participants in a church are converts. They don't have the built-in resentments toward the religion of their youth. As a result, something of the fresh, living Spirit reaches out and taps them, smiling. *Come*, it says. This is true for my cousin, Betsy. She married a Muslim and became a follower of Islam. She wholeheartedly embraced it, to the dismay of her Catholic relatives and feminist friends. They shuddered with horror at her new practices: keeping her head veiled, disappearing for prayers throughout the day, and accepting her defined role as wife and mother. Her social circle initially dwindled to practically nothing, but then expanded into the Muslim community, where her lifestyle was understood and accepted. I was intrigued and went to visit her.

Betsy and I spent a good part of the day together in her small, sunny apartment with our children. We talked about religion and our spiritual experiences.

We wiped noses and made peanut butter snacks (apparently a universal concept) for the children. At precisely noon and precisely three, she disappeared for a few minutes of devotional prayer in the direction of Mecca. She moved in her contained world with quiet grace and serene eyes, and demonstrated endless patience with her sticky, boisterous toddlers. She was happy. It was one of the most peaceful afternoons I had spent in a while, and as I took my leave my heart was full and rosy. I had been spiritually fed all day by a palpable glow of love and light that was established in the circle of their home. That day I enjoyed the mundane tasks of motherhood in a way my feminist beliefs had never allowed me to.

These days many people are turning to Earth religions for their religious expression. Ordinary Lutheran folks are attending Native American pipe ceremonies, participating in a spiral dance at a Wiccan solstice, or seeking power animals to the beat of drums in a shamanistic journey. Each of these recognizes something important: it is necessary to come once again into sacred relationship with our Mother Earth. People are turning toward religions in which God is celebrated as *immanent*, here, inside of us and the land; not *transcendent*, in a faraway place called Heaven.

This awareness is necessary for balance, but Native American leaders caution us. They don't want us to be casual about their religion, to be without real awareness and respect for it. Native elders often say to Christians, "Turn to your own roots. There is power there. There is Spirit. Go to the roots of your own religion and make it belong to you."

I took this advice and looked to my own tradition. I had maintained a connection to it in my heart, despite the fact that I hadn't been to church in years. I gave church a try, but I got a tight, contracted feeling in my stomach and chest. I trusted my body's wisdom and decided to worship somewhere else.

I'm still too eclectic to make the kind of religious commitment that Betsy chose. I've settled into a synthesis of my religious roots and my other spiritual explorations. It's big enough for breathing room and small enough for focus and consistency. It's a braid of religious practice and understanding. Each strand contributes to the power and effectiveness of the others. And they all lead me into the same circle of wholeness.

Recently, I went on a lovely retreat to a small Franciscan center run by two Catholic nuns. As I sat in their cozy living room by the fire, my eyes and heart found rest in the pictures of Jesus and Mary that hung on the walls. The sun shone like fiery jewels through a round stained glass window that depicted a female form holding up the moon. As one of the sisters moved quietly through the room, I caught the wholesome scent of almond fragrance in sesame oil. She had just given a therapeutic massage. I did not hear the click of swinging rosary beads as I used to in school, but I was reminded still of those nuns of my childhood. As I sat there, I thought of them with love. They were women with ideals and personal discipline. They were women living in community. I remembered how hard they had worked to instill the strength of religion in my soul. I realized with amazement that they had succeeded. I watched this modern sister go to the bookcase and pick up her Motherpeace tarot cards. She was going to her room to meditate near her statue of St. Francis. I watched the fire in the silent, sunlit room and realized I was home.

THE DIVINE MOTHER

We will never lose our way to the well of Her memory, and the power of
Her living flame will rise—it will rise again . . .
Celtic Goddess Chant

In ancient times, God was perceived and worshipped as female, the Divine Mother. Women were valued as leaders and contributors in society because of our close connection to the Creator through our intuition, through our connection with Nature, and through our creative and procreative abilities. Women today are leading a movement in modern society that benefits men and women alike: the rebirth of respect for the feminine principle within ourselves and in all of our institutions.

I was raised in the Catholic Church, and when I was a girl I wanted to grow up to be a priest. I remember playing "Mass" with my brothers and my friends, and always vying for that special role. I wanted to be the one who respectfully held the holy chalice aloft, and shared wise words at the sermon, the one who held her hands out in blessing at the end of the service. But I was told that I could never do that because girls were not allowed to be priests. Why? It baffled me. The boys I knew weren't even interested in the job. It was something about how Eve made a mistake a long time ago . . . or was it because Jesus's apostles were all male? What was it? I couldn't get a satisfying answer to this question, no matter how hard I tried.

I have been a seeker of truth all my life, even as a child, and I actually did pay attention in church. I listened to the priest's sermons and tried to apply the truth of what he was saying to my own life. I remember being in church one morning, standing in the back and listening to the priest speaking. I can't recall his exact words that day, but I'll never forget how deeply they wounded me. He said something casually, almost like a joke or an afterthought, about the inferiority of females. The offhand words of my parish priest insinuated that women were intrinsically weaker and spiritually less developed than men because of our gender. He said those terrible lies from the pulpit, as a spiritual authority, and no one in the congregation challenged him. I wish that someone there had leaped to their feet and called out, "Ex*cuse* me, Father! That last statement of yours was pretty sexist!" But it was 1966, and no one yet possessed the concept or the vocabulary to say that to him. His words struck my heart and my belly like a knife. A feeling of shame and rage plunged into my soul in an instant. Something shut down in me at that moment. I simultaneously closed myself off from the church, from God, and from my own female nature for many years. I count that moment as a wound to my essential self, one of the times in my development when I lost a chunk of power. I spent some effort to retrieve it when I was an adult.

But today I count myself as fortunate; I live in a time when I can heal the wounds of oppression that are specific to women. Okay, I had to do a bit of therapy about it, but no one's hauling me off to be burned at the stake anytime soon. Thanks to the most recent wave of the women's movement, women as a group have challenged the basic assumptions of what we call the patriarchy, the male-dominated mind-set that has shaped societies around the world for several thousand years. A lot has been written in the last forty years that helps us to understand the premises and ways of the patriarchal mind-set, with all the good and all the harm created through its power structures. Through the skillful scholarship of women theologians, historians, and archeologists, we can see that humanity has traveled full circle. The Divine Mother is returning to us.

A new mind-set is emerging in the West, influenced by the rise of this Divine Feminine energy—a body of informed values that is at once ancient and revolutionary. It has been incubating in circles of women since the early 1970s, and showing up shyly at workshops and conferences throughout the 1980s and 1990s. It flew off the bookshelves into the mass psyche through bestsellers like *The Mists of Avalon*, *The Red Tent*, and *The Da Vinci Code*. The modern stories of the ancient respect for the Divine Feminine offer us a memory that is also a vision: a world in which feminine strength is respected, in which we develop peaceful, ecologically sustainable societies in the unfolding millennium. This set of values has grown in definition and confidence, and now stands calmly at the doors of our institutions—churches, government, schools, and the workplace, awaiting the time for a radical shift in how things are done. Some people have called this point of view "women's spirituality," but I think it's broader than that, because many men resonate with it as well. Those of us who've followed an eclectic spiritual path for a while have an awareness of what this means, but let's get more real about it.

What exactly is the Divine Feminine spirituality? It is the cultivated awareness of God as Divine Mother, immanent in ourselves and in the Earth around us. It is a respectful consciousness of the interconnectedness of everything and the sacred honoring of all phases of created life, from birth to death. If we look at the Divine Feminine as an integrated body of spiritual values and practices, we see that it is comprised of the following characteristics:

Divine Feminine spirituality is an expression of the ancient earth-based spirituality that was widespread in human culture before the rise of the patriarchy. It is still present in Native American culture, all forms of shamanism, and in the villages of indigenous people everywhere.

Divine Feminine spirituality takes the point of view that God is immanent, or present, in the world and in our own beings. This point of view is opposite and complementary to the traditional patriarchal religious idea that God is transcendent, or beyond this world. This earth-based point of view is the balancing counterpoint to the transcendent forms of religion, which have grown "heady," too disconnected from the body and the earth.

Divine Feminine spirituality cultivates the awareness that God is female—the Divine Mother, or Goddess— as well as being God the Father, and that God guides us through feelings and intuition, as well as through reason.

❀   ❀   ❀

It assumes a Universe that is unified and benevolent, where people are essentially good. In this model, although evil exists as part of life, the duality of good and evil rests within a larger unity that is benevolent. In other words, the war between good and evil is only a small facet of what is going on in the Universe, not the main play. There is no Devil battling God to own my individual soul. Humans have no original sin; they don't need to be relieved by a church in order to be worthy citizens of Life.

❀   ❀   ❀

It is the consciousness of connection and interconnection. The goal of this way of life is to establish a state of loving respect for all of life. I foster my connection with all the communities that I become aware of: angels, people from other cultures, plants, animals—even insects. The Native Americans, with their universal sense of connectedness, referred to insects as "the little people of the air." They knew that we must peacefully coexist. This ecological consciousness was one that humans held in ancient times. Our species needs to embrace it again, wholeheartedly.

◆ ◆ ◆

Within the paradigm of Divine Feminine, time is round and cyclical, as well as linear. Time moves through the circles of the moon, the seasons, and our own bodies' clocks. Women have always been connected to "round time," linked to the cycle of the moon, and connected to the rhythm of our children's physical needs. In motherhood, life centers around the times when the baby eats, sleeps, or needs a diaper changed. We experience a stressful clash when we are forced to leave round time and our babies for many hours at linear-time jobs.

The Earth herself lives in round time, and her consciousness changes with her body's phases, responding to the pull of the moon on her tides, and her daily and seasonal alignment to the sun. People used to celebrate the Earth's time changes with rituals at spring and fall equinox and winter and summer solstice. People today who are intuitively moving back into earth-based spirituality create gatherings to do the same thing.

In this paradigm, sexuality is held as sacred. Sexuality is a healthy expression of pleasure and worship, and an act of love and celebration! We are all in the business of retrieving the gifts of that intimate experience from the repression and shame that shadows our sexuality because of centuries of distorted teachings from a misguided, patriarchal church. Sex is Nature's gift to us for procreation, but Nature must have intended it to be so much more for human beings, or she wouldn't have made it so complex and so much fun! There are so many ways we can engage in sex with another person—we're different than frogs and dogs. One of those ways is to allow it to be the ecstatic dance of God and Goddess, renewing the world again and again.

A woman's fertility and all phases of her fertility cycle are sacred, and marked with honoring ceremonies. Menstruation, sexual initiation, birth, menopause, and the advent of the wisdom of the old crone are important passages of a woman's spiritual journey. Women today are reclaiming those rites of passage from our ancient memory when the Goddess governed our lives. As more and more of us celebrate the onset of menstruation with our girls, and bring the midwife's gentle influence into our birth practices, we reinstate the glory and dignity of women's fertility. Baby Boomer women call hot flashes "power surges," and encourage each other to fearlessly express their purposes long into old age.

Fertility is a spiritual force, and I'm glad that the sacredness of fertility is starting to be restored in our culture. Growing up in America, a workaholic and productivity-driven culture, I was taught to look at menstruation as a messy inconvenience, as something that makes women flawed and less reliable as leaders. But if we look at it with sacred eyes, we might see that menstruation gives women a wisdom advantage. Our increased sensitivity to the inner self, to Nature, and the collective consciousness at those times is an opportunity for powerful meditation and steady, masterful growth. A Native American neighbor of mine still goes into her "moon lodge" when she menstruates. She stops cooking and tending her family, and retreats to her own space with a book and a journal for the first two days of her period. Her family members just pick up the slack and support her privacy; no one even questions it. Lovely! We'd be so sane if we lived in round time again as well as linear time. I think we modern women should learn about this ancient, respectful consciousness from whatever sources are available to us.

❀ ❀ ❀

A Divine Feminine point of view affirms women's traditional creative practices as spiritual practices. Creativity is an expression of the self, working with the Creator to bring new things forth. Knitting, handwork, gardening, decorating—all traditional realms that belong to women—are expressions of creativity and worthy spiritual practices if we declare them to be.

As I discussed in my previous essay, spirituality is a personal matter. Each person's spiritual truth is developed by a direct experience of God in a mystical moment and through a personal history of mystical moments. Everything I have learned about life through the lens of my female spirituality has come to me directly in a mystical moment—in an encounter with an assertive spider in the woods—as I danced ecstatically in a spiral of women singing *She changes everything She touches and everything She touches changes*—when I leaned my sweaty head on my partner's flannel shirt and felt our hearts beating together as our baby slid out of my body into a new world, sparkling with Presence—when I was struck speechless by the sight of a red maple tree strung with thousands of delicate spider webs, shimmering in bright October sunlight. My spiritual experiences as a woman are strung on a necklace of joy, bead by bead, story by story. I hope that when I lay my body down like an old husk, my spirit will rise and humbly offer this necklace at the feet of a laughing Goddess.

NOT YOUR
USUAL SPIDER

The Lord is inside you, and also inside me;
you know the sprout is hidden inside the seed . . .
Look around inside.
The blue sky opens out farther and farther,
the daily sense of failure goes away,
the damage I have done to myself fades,
a million suns come forward with light,
when I sit firmly in that world.

Kabir

I'd like to tell you a story about an experience of God's presence in the natural world. When I was in my twenties, I began a long journey out of the patriarchal religious mind-set that I was raised in. I was coming out of a period of spiritual alienation that began with a painful experience in my home church and was compounded by a sense of abandonment by God when I felt isolated by the alcoholism in our family. I was mad at God! Yet despite this, I was in a time of rapid spiritual growth. My intuition was opening up swiftly and clearly. I knew I needed to let those things go and get straight with God. I could learn how to live as a sensible and healthy mystic.

I was hot on the trail, renewing my spirituality with radically new terms. The God of my youth was an ancient, angry Father God who was jealous, cruel, judgmental, and worst of all, He had a low opinion of women! Because I was a flaming feminist in those days, I was committed to my new deity being anything but male. Although I retained a fond, abiding relationship with Jesus, I was pretty sure he wouldn't mind if I searched for a God-concept that I could relate to—one that was meaningful to me in the present. The wise part of me knew that the real God is something that is beyond male, female, or any image that human religions present to us. Inside, I intuited there was a Being with vast patience and vast generosity. It would be able to support the erratic vagaries of my human journey, as well as the cultural variety of human spiritual experience.

Eastern and Western monastic traditions agree that God can be found in nature, beauty, solitude, and contemplation. So I decided to go to the woods in search of a new experience of God. One serene summer day,

I drove out to a forest preserve. I entered the woods intending to make friends with God directly. My tolerant, nature-loving husband Fred accompanied me. When we got there, with a nod of unspoken agreement, he and I went in opposite directions down a trail, to enjoy our woodland solitude separately for a while. It was such a beautiful day. I found myself breathing deeper and dropping fully into all my physical senses as I followed the trail to a remote section of the forest. As I walked along, I became more and more aware of what I can only describe as a listening Presence in the land all around me. When I got to a little clearing that seemed friendly, I stopped and spoke out loud to the God I hoped would meet me here, deep in the woods. I said aloud: "Okay. Um . . . Hi! Please . . . show me that you are real, and show me that I can trust you."

Immediately, as if in answer to my question, there was a sudden, distinct movement in the clearing, about ten feet from me. A large spider was walking the length of a long, rotting log. When it got to the end of the log, it hopped down into the grass and began to walk across the clearing in my direction. The way that it was walking seemed curiously purposeful—very focused and direct. It walked in a straight line right toward me. Usually, insects meander and struggle a little when walking through the grass, but this was not your usual spider. It walked briskly *to* me like a tiny businessperson swinging a briefcase, and (really!) making earnest eye contact with me as it came.

As I watched the spider heading in my direction, I thought to myself, *Hmm. It's almost like that spider over there is walking over to see me. I mean, look at it—I feel like it's making eye contact with me. It really is walking over to me . . . still coming . . . getting close now, it's walking right up to my right foot. Aarghh! It's about to step onto my shoe!*

Let me explain to you right now that this was actually a very BIG spider—not your usual garden-variety daddy longlegs. *No!* This was one of those big, furry spiders with jointed limbs that you sometimes see in a remote outhouse. It scared me to death, because—I am not kidding you—this spider was as big as my fist. And its foot was on my shoe. I broke out of my paralysis and shook myself to action.

"STOP!" I shouted. "Wait a minute, spider! I am a normal human being, and I am afraid of you and I do not allow large spiders to just come over to me and walk on me!"

The spider paused and stood still. There I was in the woods, alone except for a very large spider, looking up at me questioningly with its foot upon my shoe.

As I looked down at the big hairy spider looking up at me, I realized what was happening. *Oh, my God! I've just marched into these woods and spoken to Nature with the full expectation that it would talk back to me, and here this spider walks over right away and it's touching me with its foot on my shoe—oh! Why oh why couldn't it have been a butterfly?! Did it have to be a spider? Oh, God. Okay. So it's a spider who has a spiritual message for me today.* After all, I had asked God to show me It was real and that I could trust It. I guess this is where I had to begin—with this big spider. I took a deep breath.

"All right, spider," I said. "You are part of Nature, you are part of God, and I trust you."

Immediately, the spider climbed onto my shoe and began to walk up my leg, step by rapid step, right up my calf, past my knee, up my thigh, onto my right hip. I broke out in a cold sweat of sheer terror. My heart pounded and my mind raced as I looked at this bold specimen. I could see it in detail. He really was looking right in my eyes—I wasn't making that up. I looked for colored markings, because I'd recently heard about a poisonous spider that has a violin-shaped marking on his body. *This one has a mark, but I'm not sure if it's a violin or not . . . is it one of those? Oh, God. I can't remember—do spiders attack people? Do they come after you and bite you, or only attack if they're startled and protecting their space or, or—oh, God!* I really knew nothing at all about spiders that I could draw on to comfort me or use to make a good decision in this weird situation.

"STOP, SPIDER!" I shouted. It paused, stock-still on my hip.

I did some deep breathing: full yogic breaths with my eyes closed, so I couldn't see the spider on my hip. *Okay. God is in Nature, God is in spiders, I'm talking to God today about trusting Him, God is benevolent, Nature is benevolent, neither God nor Nature wants to hurt me right now for no good reason, spiders are good, I can trust God, I can trust this spider.* This was a mystical syllogism I was inventing in the moment, desperately trying to carve out some logic in a situation that was clearly meaningful, but logical was not any part of what it was. Somehow I got myself to: *There is no good reason that this spider came all this way over here just to hurt me. What do I want to believe right now? Something about trusting God, trusting life?* I took a deep, resolved breath and said out loud, "Okay, Spider. I trust you."

Immediately, the spider left my hip and proceeded to walk right across my stomach, up my chest, and onto my right shoulder. We were undoubtedly making eye contact.

"Spider, STOP!" I yelled. I spun out into a state of high anxiety that hasn't been equaled in the thirty years since that moment. I was sweating, trembling, reviewing my life goals and purposes, and wondering if this was a good day to die. *Oh, God! There is a large hairy spider on my shoulder, and I don't know where it's going. Will it walk on my face? Can I possibly stand it if it did? On my head? If I let it onto my neck will it bite me, like a vampire? What is going to happen if I just let go and trust this thing, this situation?* In the short moment the spider rested on my shoulder, my brain sputtered and flashed its questions like sheet lightning. *Is life essentially good? Is it bad? Are there evil things out here trying to get me? Am I just nuts? Can I trust the magic of this ridiculous conversation? Will I die before my time? Are you really listening to me? Are you giving me this experience as an answer to my question about trust?* I shivered on the brink of something, alone in the woods, a spider on my shoulder.

Somehow I knew there was no way out of this experience; I had to go through it. I closed my eyes, took a deep breath, and declared, "Spider, I completely trust you."

Immediately, the spider moved again. It walked around to the back of my neck and stayed there, in a spot where I could not see it or monitor its behavior. I couldn't know if it was going to bite me. I stepped off a psychological cliff into an attitude of radical trust. I sank to the ground at the base of a tree and sat there, alone in the woods, with a large spider on the back of my neck . . . and I trusted. I *trusted*. I trusted God, the Universe, Nature, Life, myself . . . and then something happened. My sense of being a separate, individual person just dissolved. I melted into oneness with the woods, becoming part of the fabric of everything. I was aware of everything in that moment, all at once: the trees, the grasses, the breeze, the bird nearby, the spider on my neck, my heart, and the sky. I was aware of life as a seamless whole with no boundaries and no edges. No up, down, in, or out—it was all one thing, which I was an integral part of. Inside me and outside me was the same exact goodness. I sat in this divine state for a few minutes, allowing the cells of my body to be imprinted with this memory of true trust. *Life is good. God is in nature. The Universe is benevolent.*

Then it was over. My awareness shifted back to a normal sense of time and space. I spoke calmly to the spider on the back of my neck. "Spider, I am returning to the city now. I don't suppose you want to stay on me and leave this pretty place in the woods." The spider hopped off my neck and walked off into the tall grasses. It left me as purposefully as it had walked up to me, its job completed. I walked back up the trail and met my husband, who was sitting patiently on a bench, enjoying the beautiful afternoon.

He looked baffled as I spilled out my mystic's report on the experience with the spider in the woods, and said (not unkindly): "Can't you just walk in the woods on a pretty day like a normal person, and not have a wild experience?" It was early on in our relationship, so that was not yet a foolish question.

Spider is a friend of mine now, a little being who crosses my path or my vision from time to time, reminding me of my big experience of Immanence. I learned later that in the European Goddess traditions, as well as in some African and Native American tribes, spider is considered a face of the Deity—a wise and benevolent weaver of the web of life. I will always remember that day in the woods when a spider taught me that God is immanent—present in the world around me—and I am safe in this Universe because I am absolutely an integral part of it.

 Listen to Mary tell you about her encounter with the spider in an audio reading of "Not Your Usual Spider."

YOUR SPIRITUAL
TEACHER

Kabir says: Listen, friend!
My beloved Master lives inside.
Kabir

One of the basic tenets of the spiritual seeker is: my life is a classroom. I am learning an important lesson from this experience. There is a persistent hunger in many seekers to find a good spiritual teacher. I have learned that the teacher is always here, now.

When I look at my journey, I see an unbroken daisy chain of people and events that have brought me to where I stand. If I open my eyes to my circumstances today, I may recognize the class I am currently enrolled in and may feel the gentle, encouraging smile of the teacher. The teacher is always within me; it is my true Self, providing circumstances and instructors to help me grow into my own wisdom.

The amount of joy or suffering we experience in daily life is in direct proportion to the grace with which we accept our role as students. We need to recognize the course we are enrolled in, if we can, and apply ourselves to the work at hand with zest and humility. We need to give honor and thanks to the teacher. Who is our Teacher? Exactly the people and situations that we are engaged with here, now.

Relationships are teachers. My thirty-year marriage feels like a tough graduate course: Trust, Vulnerability, and Mutual Respect 300. My daughter is teaching a course: Life is Fun 101. My best friend cheerfully nudges me past the limited gates of my own thinking, and rude neighbors help me ground the principles of unconditional love and forgiveness in my life.

You can learn a lot about yourself from people who elicit a strong response from you, positive or negative. These people are mirrors for your greatness or your flaws. Study your heroes. What seedling quality in yourself is in full flower in these people? Our heroes magnetize us to them to call forth our own embryonic excellence.

All of us have someone in our environment who is irritating, someone we just love to hate. This is a teacher. There used to be a woman in my life who was very annoying, and she wouldn't go away. I bumped into her *everywhere*. After several years, I realized that this woman demonstrated the same insecurities I possessed, the ones that I had quietly hidden from myself and others. I practiced compassion and acceptance toward her as a step in greater love for myself. I don't ever see her anymore—I guess I don't need to.

Even an outright enemy is valuable. People who attack us provide us with a golden opportunity to develop more confidence, self-esteem, and boundaries. Sometimes we don't tackle these lessons unless we really need to. This is where the practice of expressing gratitude comes in. Gratitude is one of the fastest tracks to the peace and strength of the Higher Self. If we can say, "Thank you for this opportunity to become more my Self," and try to mean it, we make quick progress in the lessons taught by our adversaries.

Some people actually carry the title of "teacher." In this case, they may be real spiritual teachers or helpful technicians. A technician is someone who has a tool or technique that you can learn quickly and apply to your life to some benefit, but the actual person soon fades into the background of your life. There are a lot of technicians around these days.

Spiritual teachers—people who have truly become what they teach—are more rare. They walk their talk. It radiates from their pores. You find yourself wanting to be with them, to watch them, to hang around after class. There is something in them that you need to imprint on yourself, as a baby goose learns from its mother before it can fly. You carry these teachers in your heart all the days of your life.

I feel this way about one of my spiritual teachers. She wrote and taught about unconditional love, and in her presence, I saw unconditional love in action. It was so beautiful to watch that I felt like following her from room to room. She modeled for me the serenity and abundant energy of someone who had no inner conflicts. She served the good of the whole effortlessly, like a clear spring of water continuously bubbling forth. I suppose the fact that Edith was seventy-six and

I was thirty-one when we met accounted for her skill and insightfulness during the many times she was able to shine her wise light on my life situations. She intuitively knew how to guide my development as her student, and now that she is gone, I still look to her in my mind as I lead myself through new stages. I think her luminous clarity about my life was based on more than the fact that she was forty-five years (to the day!) older than me; I think it came as a result of her own diligence as a student of the wise teachers in her life.

The classrooms we learn the most in are difficult situations—the ones apparently not of our choosing, in which we have little external control. The urge to fret, complain, and resist is great, but we can attempt to collect ourselves and ask an important question: What spiritual principle is called for here? Patience? Tolerance? Faith? Truth? Courage? Kindness? The sooner we surrender to our assignment with willingness and zest, the sooner we can feel happy. Then, something beautiful emerges within us.

On the other hand, some learning takes a long time to unfold, and it is necessary to thrash along by trial and error. Sometimes we're in the dark without matches. We can drive ourselves mad asking, *What*

lesson is this? What am I supposed to be learning?
Don't worry—you're learning. You're just in the
process. You'll know when you know, and not before.
Just keep doing what is right in front of you with as
much love and focus as you can muster, and you can't
go too far wrong!

Sometimes we need to be in one place and allow
ourselves to be slowly and steadily opened by the hundreds of duties, challenges, and responsibilities we
take on each day. Think of this process as the opening
of a peony in June. The peony sits on its long stalk, its
life force swelling upward into a hard, round bud.
Then, along come the ants! Hundreds of tiny ants
stream up the stem and swarm all over the bud, gently
pestering the flower to uncurl her petals and let them
in to experience her nectar. For over a week, the ants
make their way inside the petals, layer after layer. They
keep tromping around, assisting the flower to open
herself fully to the sunlight. They are serving the
life force. And then one day, the peony opens—an
absolutely gorgeous flower breathing fragrance and
color into space with unabashed extravagance. If you
cut this perfect specimen and put it in a crystal vase
on your table, you will still encounter quite a few dedi-

cated ants. And like the ants in the peony, there are some lessons in our lives that will probably come in installments until the day we die—trust, vulnerability, and intimacy.

There are, however, a few courses that I know I have actually completed. I have felt my teachers smiling as they put a star on my chart. At these rare and precious times, I feel a sense of wholeness; I understand the freedom in the Native American declaration "It is a good day to die!"

MAKING FRIENDS
WITH DISCIPLINE

Keep coming back! It works if you work it.
Twelve Step slogan

Happiness is a matter of personal discipline. It is a stance that we choose; we must build and reinforce it on a daily basis whether we are in the mood or not.

Many people are allergic to the term *discipline*, perhaps because it is associated with another word: *punishment*. In truth, the practice of personal discipline is an act of self-love. It is the way we turn our backs on a long, bleak history of abandonment and come home to ourselves. Making friends with discipline is one of the best things we can do for ourselves.

A recovering alcoholic employs discipline to get to an AA meeting, even though she doesn't feel like it. A man who was abused by his parents halts his knee-jerk response to hit his own rebellious child, even though he feels as if he wants to. We may initially turn to self-discipline because our lives have become unmanageable, but discipline can become our lifelong ally if we are serious about our spiritual journey.

Spiritual mastery will come to us as a result of becoming disciplined on all levels of the personality—physical, emotional, and mental. On the physical level, this means establishing good health habits, being financially responsible, keeping beauty and order in our environment, and walking in balance with the natural world. On the emotional level, it means handling feelings appropriately. We need to know how and when to feel, express, and release emotions, as well as when to detach from excessive sensitivity. On the mental level, it is our responsibility to uproot negative, conditioned beliefs in our minds and to cultivate a positive, self-chosen worldview.

Ultimately, we are meant to be the masters of our minds, not servants—to focus our thoughts or be silent at will. This discipline is the goal of meditation. As we make progress, our personalities become clean and luminous, so the inner Spirit can shine through. We can operate with more and more love and power, for the well-being of everyone. This is a long-term project, but I can't think of a better way to spend life.

Usually, it is obvious what area of our lives calls for self-discipline. We feel out of control, frustrated, and ashamed. Maybe we are denying the problem, even though we get consistent feedback from others that our lack of self-control is problematic for *them*. We are then asked to make a change that feels unnatural to us. In his book *The Road Less Traveled*, M. Scott Peck describes discipline as an "unnatural" act. It is certainly a radical act of the spiritual will. We make a commitment to an upward trend in our lives and choose new attitudes or behaviors.

At first it feels like pushing a boulder uphill. We make infinitesimal, erratic progress for a while, but this is deceptive—a lot of growth is going on underground. It is better to make some small, real changes than to make a big, heroic, noisy effort for several days, completely forget about our commitment, and then backslide. That adds to our original hopelessness about our ability to change.

Practicing a new discipline without being attached to immediate results works best. We will make incremental progress and leave crisis behind. If we persist in our effort, we will begin to stabilize. We will gain glimpses of our mastery of this part of our lives. It is common at this point to want the "reward" of relaxing our discipline—and then comes the backslide! The painful fact remains that we must follow persistence with *more* persistence *and* vigilance. The old patterns of behavior have long, tough roots into our beings, and have been dominant for many years. But if we continue to do what is good for us whether we feel like it or not, we build a new foundation that can last for the rest of our lives. Repetition has a power that realigns the patterns in our unconscious and allows us to become different creatures.

Currently, my discipline is aimed at keeping my desk clean and organized. I grew up in alcoholic chaos, and disorder is a real dragon for me. The sight of a pile of papers to file elicits feelings of hopelessness and being overwhelmed. But the beat goes on—my past successes assure me that I can become more organized, despite my old emotions. A few years from now, it will seem natural to have an orderly desk— another star on my chart.

The Ten Steps to Discipline:

1. **Acknowledge the need to become more disciplined in how you live your life.** Crack through any denial about your out-of-control behavior. Make the distinction between discipline and punishment—discipline is an act of love. Deal with the emotions of rebelliousness.

2. **Seek inspiration.** Most of the world's great leaders and performers have had tremendous personal discipline. Who are your heroes? Hang up their pictures. Let their excellence call you forward to realize your own aims.

3. **Decide to become disciplined.** Choose an area where there is a crying need. State your will to make a change with the help of your Higher Self. Say it aloud as a statement of your spiritual will: "I will become neat and organized." "I will become honest with myself and others." "I will finish what I start." "I will take the time to cook a good meal."

4. **Enlist support.** Choose friends who demonstrate personal discipline and learn from them. Tell your current friends and family that you are making some difficult changes and that you want their quiet, nonjudgmental support for your effort. Talk to your Higher Self about it often.

5. **Release feelings of hopelessness.** Hopelessness *will* come up when you attempt to change long-standing patterns. Feel it, cry or rage about it, but don't *believe* it anymore. Keep moving.

6. **Stay on track.** Remind yourself every morning what your discipline is. Remember that it isn't optional. Do it. Post a copy of your spiritual will statement where you can see it. At night, review the day. Did you do what you needed to do today to produce long-term happiness? Check in with a friend about it at least once a week.

7. **Acknowledge your progress.** Celebrate glimpses of health and accomplishment in your chosen area of discipline.

8. **Persist, persist, persist.** Acquire a taste for repetition and good habits.

9. **Stabilize in your new mode.** Give yourself time to get used to new behaviors. Remember that they're

still new. It can take years to stabilize, but your work is worth it. You are building a new foundation for your life.

10. **Be vigilant!** Notice if you're relaxing your practices. Notice what happens to you and your life when you do. Remember the power of repetition. Try not to be compulsive or rigid, but remember that too much relaxation isn't a treat for you—it is self-abandonment.

THE SERENITY PRAYER—
IT'S ALL THERE

God, grant me the serenity to accept the things I cannot change,
the courage to change the things I can,
and the wisdom to know the difference.

The Serenity Prayer

The Serenity Prayer is an indispensable part of every Twelve Step gathering. It contains the sum total of what spiritual life is: a series of lessons about when to accept life as it is, and when to make changes for the better. You can say this prayer thousands of times and still find it meaningful; at any given time we need to employ acceptance, courage, or wisdom to feel peace of mind in the moment. In the early years of recovery we must employ these concepts mindfully, but eventually they become part of our beings.

In a way, this prayer is a global contemplation: the wisdom of East and West meets here. Eastern wisdom teaches us to accept life. There is nowhere you have to go; it's all right here. Everything you see is equally One, an expression of God's consciousness in myriad forms. Be at peace with what you are, here, now. Accept. Western wisdom says, "You can be something more than you are right now—strive for it! Life can be better. You can use your knowledge and will to make changes that advance evolution. There is no problem that cannot be solved, and no creative innovation is beyond your reach. Courage!"

It is the wisdom of the Whole that knows which wisdom must predominate now, though each is bound to the other, inseparable partners in the dance of creation through time.

The truth in the Serenity Prayer must be horse sense because even my little daughter understood it. She gave me a fine lesson one night. I was in a stew about something and she said, "Is there anything you can do about that?"

I thought about it and replied that I couldn't.

"Well then, Mom, I guess you'll just have to enjoy your own life," she told me matter-of-factly.

How did she figure that out at such a young age? There were thousands of adults all over the nation struggling to fix everything wrong or feeling unable to make any changes in their lives. I guess she never "unlearned" her basic wisdom.

Those of us who grew up in dysfunctional homes need the basic wisdom of the Serenity Prayer. We are out of balance most of the time because we are not accepting life as it is. We are not confidently using our wills to make the changes that can make our lives better. We live trying lives.

Several years ago my Inner Self told me, "You must give up *trying*."

Trying what? I wondered. Before long I began to realize that "trying" had been my baseline approach to life and that it was extremely stressful. I had been *trying* for so long—trying to win my dad's admiration, trying to save my family of origin from alcoholic collapse, trying to be liked.

Trying is the opposite of peace and success. We have to accept life as it is *and* use our skillful, spiritual wills to open our lives to their fullest potential. Period. No more trying. *Commitment* to living this paradox brings serenity and excellence to a human life.

How do you gain acceptance of life as it is? Get to know and accept yourself, train your abilities, and then use them in service to others. Accept your duties, accept others, accept the miracle of new life, and accept the mystery of death. Accept the challenges of your generation and its contribution to society. Acceptance grows in an incremental way, like the ring of new wood that a tree gains each year.

It's harder when you have to dig yourself out of crippling childhood pain. But the years bring maturity and acceptance, if we are open to it. Life itself teaches acceptance of life. Eventually, we learn certain lessons. Nobody's perfect, especially me. I can't keep anybody; people change, die, or move away. When a relationship is over, no matter how much love there was, it's over. I can't keep anything; things get lost, worn, outdated.

As we continue to mature, acceptance is no longer a thought or a process; it is a relaxed, open state of being. It is the state of being empty and full simultaneously, established in the present, and a container of positive potential in every moment, for everyone.

Free and powerful human beings—enlightened masters—live in this manner. These saints have become established in the acceptance of life. They are radiant lights of peace, love, and joy, regardless of their environment or circumstances. The will of their personalities is so powerfully aligned with the Divine Will that miraculous things are accomplished through them all the time, with no effort. No trying! They enhance the liberation of other people with calm detachment. They are able to see perfection in imperfection! The Serenity Prayer contains this bright human potential in seedling form.

GIVING AND
RECEIVING

For it is in giving that we receive.

St. Francis

The ability to genuinely give and receive is a challenge for many of us. This is especially true if we grew up in environments that were painfully out of balance in terms of healthy giving and receiving. Some people learned to give-give-give as a way of feeling valued and important. Others learned to take everything they could get—more than their share—in an attempt to fill a gaping hole inside. As adults, these people often get into relationships with each other and engage in a frustrating dance of immature love that ends in alienation, guilt, and blame. In fact, both types of people, the ones who give too much and the ones who take too much, bear the same wound: the wound of the needy child.

Very few people in our world get all of their childhood needs met. (We are all part of the world's largest dysfunctional family—the human race!) Children need to be raised by a centered pair of grown-ups, along with the support of an extended family and a community. They need to be protected, nourished, appreciated, and guided as they unfold their potential. However, many families offer only a modicum of protection and "three hots and a cot"—and some children don't even get that.

If our needs are not met as children, we become perpetually needy. As adults we may adapt to these unmet needs by becoming reckless givers with an exaggerated sense of responsibility toward others. We may have an inability to receive, even if what we need is staring us right in the face. Or we may become selfish and self-absorbed, unable to respond to the needs of others without feeling resentful and taken advantage of. We may have both of these attitudes in different areas of our lives.

Being human means having needs and having to meet the needs of others. There is no way around it. No one who is unable to give and receive comfortably has recovered. It's like breathing. You can't just breathe out constantly without breathing in—you'll die. Neither can you take in the air and withhold your carbon dioxide from the environment. You have to give that back. A healthy person is meant to be constantly giving and receiving in an easy, steady rhythm, exactly like breathing. Breathe in, breathe out. Breathe in, breathe out. Receive, give. Receive, give. Simple. For adult children of dysfunctional families, this basic function must be regained by steady self-healing. Fortunately, we can do this simply by being ourselves.

It is human nature to yearn toward wholeness. Even when you are choosing the wrong people and situations, replaying your original wounds, you are attempting to heal yourself. Subconsciously, you choose people and situations that resemble your family. You might think, *If only I try hard, I can fix this person and then he or she will meet my needs.* It never works that way. You cannot successfully fill a need frozen from the past by controlling someone in the present. You can never do it "right enough." The person will tire of you, leaving you with your gaping hole and a fresh wound to lick.

To heal the needy child within, turn your face continuously to the nourishing presence of the Higher Self. You can accept God as Mother and Father and entrust your needs, your vulnerability, and your innocence to a parent who won't let you down. This Spirit will provide you unfailingly with people and circumstances to heal your wounds, meet your needs, and bring you into balance. It wants to help you move into greater harmony! In exchange, all you need is to receive willingly what is coming to you and give what life is asking you to give.

Many people are afraid to receive. They feel guilty or afraid they don't deserve something good, especially when they haven't asked for it. Or they fear they are depriving someone else by accepting something. Some people are afraid to receive because they believe they will become vulnerable to manipulation or be "in debt" to the giver. It takes right understanding and healthy self-esteem to be able to receive the goodness life is capable of giving us. This understanding and self-esteem can be gained in increments if you are willing to s-t-r-e-t-c-h open to it, a bit at a time. A local teacher refers to this ability to receive and retain life's goodies as a "level of having-ness."

It takes trust and vulnerability to receive good things—you have to be willing to be open to the unexpected. You may need to acknowledge that someone else really sees you and cares enough to serve your needs *freely*. I have a neighbor who is a single mother of seven kids, all living at the poverty line. Every time she sees me she tells me how exhausted she is. Yet when I sincerely offer my help, she refuses it. I finally realized that she is unwilling to be vulnerable to me and my caring. She wants to struggle along with what is familiar and complain about it; she doesn't want to open up her heart to human compassion. Why? Maybe because she'll cry. Sometimes you need to cry in order to receive. You need to feel and release old pain instead of running from it. People who are more interested in transformation than total control will walk forward, into unfamiliar realms of greater good, even as they tremble with fear and uncertainty.

The ability to genuinely give also requires a right understanding. You have probably experienced the sweet exhilaration and openness of true giving at times. At other times, you may have felt drained or resentful afterward. Why would giving make you feel this way? You might have felt drained for one of three reasons:

1. **You were giving with a motive and an attachment to a certain outcome or response from the other person.** This is *not* giving, it is manipulation.
2. **You were giving to someone who was *taking*, but not able to receive.** Think about that one for a while.
3. **You were giving beyond what was really practical for you to do.** Our time, energy, and resources are valuable. A certain amount of control is necessary.

Imagine that you are sitting in a cafe when an acquaintance sits down to tell you her problems. It is practical for you to lend a helping hand, so you choose to do that. Giving and receiving take place, and you both feel good about the encounter. If, however, your purpose in sitting in the cafe is to be alone with your own thoughts, you cannot really give to your acquaintance when she sits down to talk. You need to be true to your own intentions and inform her in an openhearted way that you don't want to talk to anyone right now. Your honesty is the best gift to both of you at that moment.

There are times when we are able to stretch our capacity for giving way beyond practical limits. Certain special situations call forth a wellspring of love and service. We perceive that all giving is receiving: there is only one Self, who is both the servant and the recipient of that same love. This is the highest perception, one that a serious spiritual seeker can eventually attain. Mother Teresa was asked, "How could you have personally picked up thousands of dying bodies from the streets of Calcutta?" She replied, "I have only lifted One."

EVERYTHING'S NOT
UNDER CONTROL

Life is what happens to you while you're busy making other plans.

John Lennon

"**Y**ou're so controlling!" I can't tell you how many times I have heard my husband exclaim this in exasperation. Adult children of alcoholics like me are notorious for attempting to control people and things in their environment.

My poor husband is often at the wrong end of my controlling behavior. I want to monitor how much he works, how much television he watches, and how he does his job as a father. He *should* be paying more attention to *me*. I also want to control my daughter—

what she eats and what she wears. She *must* be healthy and socialized.

Doesn't reading that make you tense? I must be tense whenever I am controlling. It seems to me, now, that the need to feel in control is essentially a by-product of lacking trust in life. When I am controlling, I am trying to make everything all right because I *don't* know and *don't* trust that everything really *is* all right. I need to go to a new level of faith and trust in my Higher Power. This means coming into right relationship with "control."

The correct exercise of control is such a human dilemma. As a species, humans love control. We want to control our environment, physical and emotional safety, financial security, and self-image. We want to control others or be controlled by them. We create roles, habits, rules, and personal and political systems that reflect our need to control. We're good at this, and a lot of it is necessary to establish basic order and a healthy status quo. Yet this same passion for control gets us into trouble as individuals and as a species. If we do not exercise wisdom, control can easily become addiction, tyranny, and repression. We find ourselves rebelling against excessive control with a cry of "Freedom!" We take refuge in creative chaos. Yet if we are serious about manifesting our ideas in the world around us, we need to re-create some structure that doesn't stifle or control us.

If you are serious about discovering and fulfilling your purpose, you must establish a right relationship with control on every level of your being: physical, emotional, mental, and spiritual. Having some control over your world is a foundation upon which to dance with life's spontaneity.

Life's creative unpredictability is both unsettling and delicious. We really have no control over most of it. But we can trust life anyway, if we come into a correct relationship with control on an emotional level. There's nothing you can't handle—as long as you can have your feelings and share them with others. People, jobs, and homes will come and go in your life, bringing up lots of feelings. Everyone has a cache of buried pain, waiting to erupt to the surface, asking for healing. Our organism is always yearning toward health and wholeness, and our life situations will repeat the drama of our early wounds until we fully feel and heal them.

One of the common traits of addiction is the desire to control and repress the experience of painful emotions. Spending time and money on an addictive substance or a project that prevents you from feeling painful emotions restricts you in your life; your mind and body will become more rigid and less adaptable as you age. However, if you realize that your pain is a gift, and if you are determined to trust life, you can use your time and resources to feel your pain and heal from it, instead of avoiding it with an addiction. Some people need to exert more control over their feelings because they are awash in emotion. They need to learn to contain their feelings and discipline themselves to bring focus to their bodies, minds, and spirits.

You always have one power that no one can take away from you: the power to change your point of view. This is the way to have control on a mental level. We cannot control life, but we *can* cancel our expectations. We can accept that, in some inexplicable way, all is well—even when things are *not* going as we expect them to. This is an empowering perspective you can adopt in any circumstance. It will keep you from slipping into a victim role.

I met a woman the other day who really understands this. She is so alive and excited about her journey and the mysterious, inevitable unfolding of God's plan for her life. Last year she suddenly lost her job of eighteen years in a company reorganization. Instead of blaming her superiors, she could hardly keep from smiling and exulting. God must have a wonderful surprise in store, to move her along so abruptly!

The insecurity most people have about their jobs could be a blessing in disguise. Previously stable companies are merging, disappearing, and reincarnating all over the place, forcing thousands of people to abandon their belief in an external source of control and security. These people must turn to inner resources of serenity amid a sea of change. They are starting to listen to spiritual impulses for a new direction in their lives. Security always has been a very temporal thing, subject to change. Serenity in the face of the fluctuation of the things that are beyond our control is a much more precious commodity—and we can always choose to have it.

This is *self-control*. Self-control on a spiritual level means being willing to let go of control and follow our spiritual impulses. This is different from the scattered, uninformed impulsiveness of an immature person who is afraid to think through consequences. It is different from compulsion, which is rigid, repetitive, and familiar. Our inner being constantly communicates its desire and direction through spontaneous impulses.

These impulses come to us as a flash in our mind's eye. We might hear a little voice in our minds saying, *Why don't you . . . ?* At times it is an unself-conscious, compassionate reaching out to touch someone we hardly know. When we act upon divine impulse, we step across the gap of the unknown into a new realm. Like a mountain climber in the crystalline air, we exist only in the present moment. We have a quiet mind and relaxed concentration. For a moment, we suspend judgment and concerns about outcomes and follow our impulse with trust and detachment. This willingness to walk through the doorway of possibility brings adventures to life. We open up to receive from God more than we can imagine creating on our own. With spiritual self-control, we can contain this goodness and continue strengthening our foundation to hold even more.

LIVING IN
CONTENTMENT

Don't worry!
Whatever is supposed to happen will happen—it never fails!
Face everything contentedly while absorbing your mind in God.
Lalleshwari

I've got a problem. What will I do? I have been on a journey of self-healing for many years. It started when I observed that I was creating wreckage and trouble for people I wanted to be close to. I have made a lot of progress. I am no longer inappropriate or irresponsible. I am trustworthy toward myself and others. I have even accomplished some goals and gained respect in my community. My problem is that my journey has brought me to the borders of an unfamiliar country: Contentment.

Long ago, I heard about this country and decided it was a dangerous place, one to be avoided. Wasn't it bland, boring, and mind-numbing there? Didn't Contentment seduce you into forgetting your responsibility to solve the world's problems? Wouldn't I lose my passion, my intensity, and my identity as a heroic fighter, *trying* to beat unbeatable odds? My ancestors came from a country called Struggle; who was I to leave my heritage and take up residence in the alien lands of Peace and Plenty?

Being content is a tough, aesthetic choice that I am intentionally making in my life. If there was a painting of the psychological landscape of my childhood amid alcoholism and of my young adult years, it would look like a masterpiece sprung from the brush of American painter Jackson Pollock. Chaotic swirls, intensity of color and movement . . . murky hints of evil and destruction . . . shock and struggle, screeching rebelliously from the canvas: "Life! Freedom!" Whew. Pretty interesting, but hard to live there for long.

I turn to the painting of the landscape that seems to beckon to me now. It looks like it was painted by Paul Cezanne. Small homes nestle cozily among quiet hills and trees in perfect balance. The land, painted in soft tones, is watered by calm rivers of meaning and interconnection with others. It is not without interest. Look! A large swan flaps upward from the inlet where it was hiding. Can I choose this peaceful valley of Contentment? Not yet. I need to understand more about what "contentment" means before I do.

One thing I have learned is that experiencing contentment in a situation has nothing to do with the *content* of the situation. Contentment is an attitude, a choice about where I will focus my attention. A situation can change completely, but you can remain just as unhappy with an attitude of discontent.

I learned this by going on vacation. Most summers, I tend to chafe and moan about living on a big, hot city block. Garbage and broken glass litter the street. Any time, day or night, there is a cacophony of barking dogs, honking horns, and drunken fights. This offends my innate preferences for beauty and quiet. My family is not in a position to move somewhere else, so it is very easy to get mad and miserable about living here.

One summer, I thought I would be able to bear it if we could retreat to the quiet woods for two weeks.

I arranged a cabin-on-a-lake-at-a-small-family-resort vacation and comforted myself all summer by glancing at the last two weeks of August, outlined in marker on the kitchen calendar. At last the day came, and we made our the escape.

Well, it was *quiet*. But the cabin was dark, smelly, and claustrophobic. Tacky pictures covered the walls. The tap water was golden brown. It rained for two days and then remained cloudy and muggy for a few more. There were flies and mosquitoes in the air and a terrifying rumor of leeches in the lake. During the long days indoors, my daughter played her Sesame Street tape over and over. My husband repetitively played Indian raga music. I began to thrash and writhe in discontent. I became a pollutant in our small cabin environment, so toxic that my husband and daughter sought refuge in games of solitaire and visiting with other families. After several days of this, I decided to salvage the remnants of my self-respect and discipline myself into contentment. It wasn't easy, but the other choice appeared to be another week of misery and my increasing unpopularity with my family.

In order to achieve a better attitude, I sat down with a notebook. I made a list of things I would have preferred about this vacation: sweet clean water, airy rooms, sunny days, and no leeches. I allowed myself to fully savor each preference while telling myself that I would no longer *expect* these things. My expectations and attachments were causing me to suffer. I heaved a big sigh and wrote the reasons why being at the cabin was a gift and a blessing. I listed everything positive that had occurred so far. Without trying very hard, my list of positives outweighed the negative list, two to one. I expressed gratitude for these things and shifted my focus of attention for the rest of the week. We had a good time.

I was reminded that every circumstance has a front and a back. My contentment lies in my ability to choose the focus of my attention. Some people say that contentment is "wanting what you have." I now see that, in any given situation, *some goal of mine is being fulfilled*. I am not a victim of anything. I may not perceive that I am getting what I need because I have both short-term and long-term goals in operation. There are times when some of my goals are on hold while others are being fulfilled. I think that the art of contentment lies in the ability to perceive how I am reaping what I have asked for.

Four years ago, I earnestly asked God to give me complete and unshakable self-esteem. I heard an inner voice say, "Fine. You've got it. It will take you five years to attain that." Ever since then, I have been in situations that directly nurtured my self-esteem or challenged it to the roots. In difficult scenarios, I choose to see that God is answering my prayer and giving me an opportunity to gain on my goal.

In the case of my stressful urban environment, I was not meeting my short-term goal of getting a good night's sleep. But I was meeting my short-term goal of living cheaply, so I didn't have to work long hours. I had lots of family and leisure time that I wouldn't have had if I were struggling to make a large mortgage payment. I was also being forced to work on some important long-term spiritual goals: cultivating *inner* peace and developing enough humility to see God in all people. It was my choice to learn to *see* my city block as the best learning laboratory to achieve these golden goals. **The process of living in contentment is threefold:**

1. The experience of healthy discontent arises when we have practical or spiritual needs that must be met.

2. We create short- or long-term goals to meet our needs and observe contentedly the manner in which the goals are realized.
3. We need to be realistic about the impermanence and unpredictability of life. We must be willing to let go of each and every one of our desires when it is time.

◈ ◈ ◈

I was once crying to God about how betrayed I felt; I was bitterly aware that all the people I love could be taken away from me, and ultimately, I have no control. I heard that inner voice say, "I haven't let you down. I never told you that you could keep anybody. It's not part of the deal here."

Everything is impermanent: jobs, homes, people, and your body. Each of these things is merely a container that holds what you fill it with—love or fear. The containers are continuously invented. We maintain them for a while, and then they either gently deteriorate or abruptly break apart. Imagine! What if you approached your whole life with the delight and detachment you feel sitting in the sun, blowing soap bubbles from a toy wand? When you set out to blow bubbles, you fully expect them to be imperma- nent, yet you do it anyway. You want to see how many you can make at once, how big they can be, how long they last, and how they will eventually break. You treasure each rainbow-streaked sphere for as long as it lasts, confident that there will always be more, as long as you choose to play.

This is my painting of contentment. I will not choose the painting of the quiet valley by Cezanne. There could always be bulldozers in the future. Instead, I choose a painting that shows a sweet-faced person sitting on a mountain, blowing bubbles into the air. The person seems innocent, comfortably vul- nerable to life. Perhaps it takes a certain amount of deliberate innocence to live a life of contentment these days. The lofty perch on the mountain gives the person just the right perspective on things. Face-to- face with the Creator, this person creates beautiful, delicate bubbles that grace the world for a while and then pass on their way—as the Creator does with each one of us.

A WILD TRUST

In wildness is the preservation of the world.
Henry David Thoreau

"I don't know what I *need!*" I cried out in frustration one day. I was facing one of the great dilemmas for a person with low self-esteem: a positive opportunity. I had just received a respectable settlement from a five-year court battle, and now I had enough resources to make choices beyond maintaining my family's status quo and paying monthly bills. Since childhood, I was acclimated to struggle, so the arrival of an opportunity for choice and ease was so foreign that it was stressful. Strangely, it made me depressed.

"I know what you need," one of my friends suggested. "Just trust me on this."

A week later, I was on my way to a five-day treatment center for family members of alcoholics. On the first day, my counselor said a few simple things that uncorked a river of tears that flowed without interruption for most of the time I was there. I allowed myself to be herded along from group to group. I learned to see my crisis orientation as a fallout effect of my father's disease. I grieved the loss of childhood, and the physical and emotional neglect I experienced as a child. By the end of the program, a significant change had taken place in me. I went home with a small but sturdy understanding that I am a worthy person who deserves to have what she needs.

But what were my needs? Should I move out of the inner city to a quieter neighborhood? Take that trip to Ireland? Go to art school? I didn't know. I started by looking at different neighborhoods. I looked for a few months, but always found myself saying the same thing: "It's not quiet enough to warrant the trouble of moving, and there aren't enough trees." Was I being a perfectionist? Even the premier neighborhoods in my city were not quiet enough or pretty enough for me.

One day my best friend called up and said, "Let's go to the meditation program tonight. I feel really drawn to it, so I bet it'll be a good one." We went and it was nice—nothing stellar. But after the program I spoke to a woman about my house search and she said, "I don't know why I'm telling you this, but there is this piece of land that I know of. The owner needs to sell it. He might have even sold it to the government already, but I think you should go see it."

"What the heck," I thought. "It's May. A beautiful time for a field trip."

So Fred and I followed the lead and made arrangements to see the land, even though the owner thought the government was going to buy it soon. The land was located on the St. Croix River, in an area almost completely surrounded by forest. There were only seven permanent dwellings in a ten-mile radius. We left the pavement and the farms behind and crunched for miles down a long gravel road. As we passed a field, a black shape caught my attention. It wasn't a cow.

"Fred, stop!" I cried, "That's a bear!"

We stopped the car. The bear ambled through the sunny field right toward us, his blue-black fur gleaming with health. He was the spirit of relaxation itself,

His whole manner communicated the ease of a wild thing who feels safe in his habitat. He was mellow. When he saw us, he loped away into the brush.

"A bear! A *bear*!" I was beside myself with simple, mindless joy. My whole being was energized. I remembered what a friend predicted for me during our Spring Equinox meditation. *You are going to meet a wild animal this year, and it's going to awaken a part of you that you have forgotten about. It's going to change your life.* I couldn't imagine what she meant then, but I could feel a big change happening now.

When we got to the property, Fred said, "I have the strangest feeling that I'm coming home."

We toured the house and its forty acres, accompanied by Dan, the son of the owner, Dick. In a way, the visual appearance of the land was unremarkable. The forest was bare and scruffy. The sandy soil could only support jack pines, birches, and oaks. Things grew slowly there, and fell down if they got too big. This barren pine forest and grassland had a desert quality. But there was something remarkable shimmering within every blade of grass. This place was saturated with a palpable feeling of love. The garden, the birdhouses, and the tubs of water for the deer to drink from—all spoke of the owner's deep appreciation for nature. Beneath and beyond his relationship with it, the place was infused with wildness.

As the three of us entered a large field under the open sky, I was embarrassed to find myself nodding off into a trance. I excused myself and went off to sit alone in the middle of the field. I went into a deep meditation there, the kind I have only experienced a few times in holy places. In the silence, I could sense the heart of the Earth beneath me. I could feel her consciousness breathing from her center to the outer stratosphere.

"Here," I thought, "she still breathes deeply—unencumbered by cement and human inventions."

All potential obstacles melted before us. Dick and his wife, Viola, decided that Fred and I should be the next stewards of their beloved land. They withdrew the deal from the government. When I met Dick and Viola for the first time in the bank lobby, I wanted to proceed with dignity, but instead I burst into uncontrollable tears of happiness.

"There, there," Viola said, patting me and offering me a tissue. "You're going to have many wonderful years there, just like we did."

She held my hand in her wrinkled one as I quietly snuffled and hiccoughed as the papers were passed around the table. It was a four-tissue signing, and everyone was damp-eyed by the time we were done. We went out to lunch to celebrate. I was touched to learn how much this land meant to Dick. He tried to tell us so many things about it, but his sentences trailed off in confusion. His mind had been crippled by a stroke, forcing him to leave the woods and move to town, near his children.

"I used to be so smart, so strong. I could do any-thing. I'm just a dunce now! I don't like who I am anymore."

"Oh, Dick," Viola said, "Now, don't talk like that."

"I see that you really hate these limitations," I said. "I don't blame you for feeling like you do."

Six days later, Dick died. He succumbed quickly to an undiagnosed heart condition. His family had a small service in his home; Fred and I were the only ones who were not immediate family. Looking around the crowded living room, I had the eerie feeling that I already knew every one of these strangers. They embraced us as their own. I stood up during the speak-ing part of the service and thanked the family for bringing so much love to the land over the years. When I invited them to walk there any time they wished, the entire group heaved a collective sigh of relief. They had lost Dick, but they wouldn't have to lose his land.

During the course of the evening everyone came up to us one by one to tell us their favorite stories. The time the bear came to the window . . . the time Mother saw the black snake and made the neighbor move it and he fainted . . . the deer who brought her new fawns to show Dick because he was her friend . . . the night they saw the UFO. I collected their stories in my heart like the wild spring strawberries they'd gathered in baskets when they were children. My child and her friends will gather them now.

We lingered outside in the sunset when it was time to go, reluctant to dissolve the experience of unexpected community. Suddenly, a large monarch butterfly flew from the doorway of the house. It went right between my head and Fred's, beating a straight path for the horizon. It flew with a strength and focus that seemed uncharacteristic of a butterfly.

"Fred, that's Dick!" I knew his spirit was saying a joyous farewell. I sensed the completion of his passage, and the freedom he enjoyed after leaving his body.

My land has been my healer. Season by season, year after year—it nurtures a new trust in life that is growing in my heart. For now, we straddle two worlds, inner city and remote country. It is a perfect balance. I feel safe in the woods, in a place so silent that you can hear the wind coming to you long before it reaches your face. We have seen eagles, hawks, porcupines, beavers, deer, all sorts of birds, a few snakes, and two more big black bears. The sight of a wild creature living in its own way fills me with excitement that lasts for days. I feel so much joy when I am walking in the scruffy woods and stumble across a hole that is a doorway to someone's home. Whose? Fox? Badger? I tell myself to remember these footprints, and look them up.

One weekend, Fred was on the property by himself. He told me that he found himself being guided from place to place around the forty acres, and at each place he found traces of Dick's unfinished odds and ends. "It's just uncanny," he said. "It's like he's here showing me around."

That night I dreamed of Fred walking and working the land, a large monarch butterfly resting on his forehead.

INTUITION

(now the ears of my ears awake and the eyes of my eyes are opened)

e. e. cummings

"I don't know. It's just a gut-level feeling." "It's just a hunch." "It's women's intuition." It's funny how dismissively we talk about that quiet knowing that comes right out of our souls. That's what intuition is—the prompting of our souls to take the paths that will bring us the highest good in our lives. It speaks to us in different ways. To some people it is the "still, small voice" within. To others, intuition comes as a picture in the mind, in either the waking state or the dream state. It can be a gut-level feeling, a sense of emotional comfort or discomfort. It can be a flash of full-blown knowing that drops suddenly into our consciousness, bringing information or inspiration from out of the blue.

Unfortunately, most of us repress our intuition, insisting that it be subordinate to our logical minds. We regard intuition as an unsettling, embarrassing second cousin to logic, control, and linear thinking—functions we have been trained to rely on. We ignore intuition's suggestions for so long, it either atrophies into total silence or finds loud, dramatic ways of getting through to us. Sometimes we don't listen to what we know until our life goes off the road in a messy crisis, forcing us to give up our reliance on the logical "shoulds."

Your intuition is trying to show you only one thing all the time: how to be happy as you. It's there to make life easier. Your intuition will help you understand your purpose, unfold it, and solve everyday problems. It needs to be reinstated on its throne next to the logical mind, so the two can work as partners.

Your intuition transmits visions for a life-direction that will make you happy, using your unique nature to the fullest. Your planning mind makes a strategy. But it can't make an airtight strategy because there are always unknowns. Your intuition works through these unknowns, bringing ideas and resources into play in the present moment. Your logical mind organizes information. It balances your checkbook. Your intuition balances your life. It tells you about health needs, connects you with good friends, and helps you with timing. It leads you into situations that elicit joy. Together, your intuition and logical mind create a fulfilling, effective life.

Intuition operates in large and small ways. A number of years ago, my intuition showed me in a dream that I needed to relocate to a different city as soon as possible. My logical mind was appalled and embarrassed; I had no reason to move. I had to finish school in my hometown. I had a lot of friends and family who would be sad and mystified by my move. But my feeling was strong, so I did it. I met my beloved husband in a grocery store on my first venture into town. We fell in love instantly. Also, my health improved dramatically. I had been sick with a variety of complaints for almost two years. I discovered that I was a creature at odds with my old environment, and that I could be more relaxed and healthy in my new location.

My intuition helps me with smaller challenges, too. While I was driving around on errands, my little voice said, *Go home right now*. My logical mind told me I needed to go to the store first. *Really, right now. Go home*. My logical mind whined as I turned toward home—prematurely, as far as it was concerned. As I entered my front door, the phone was ringing. It was a person I had tried to get in touch with unsuccessfully for two weeks. We made a quick little transaction that eased my current work project, and I went back out, smiling.

How to Strengthen Intuition

Acknowledge that it's there. Even if it has atrophied from disuse, your intuition can be awakened and brought back into your life. Talk to it. Say, "I know you're there. I'd like you to be working in my life. Please become active for my highest good."

Notice how your intuition speaks to you. Do you hear a little voice that is almost like the rest of your thoughts, but not quite? Do you see pictures in your mind? Do you know things but doubt that you know them because you don't have actual proof? Does your body give you clues about whether certain people are trustworthy? Discover which of these modes is strongest and focus on it.

Take some risks. Start small. Follow your little hunches instead of your conditioned brain. See where your energy *wants* to go, not where you think it *should* go. Do something because it feels right, not because it makes sense. Follow your spiritual impulse.

Trial and error. Good discrimination between the intuitive mind and the conditioned mind takes time and practice. Don't doubt everything just because you're wrong sometimes. *Decide* to be accurate with intuition and keep practicing.

Become willing to flow more in your life. Let your life be easier. Cultivate an appetite for synchronicity and surprise. Being in control all the time is exhausting and unimaginative. Let the creativity of the Universe into your life. Enjoy!

HUMILITY

We ask ourselves, who am I to be brilliant, gorgeous, talented, fabulous?
Actually, who are you not to be? You are a child of God.
Marianne Williamson

Many years ago, when I started therapy, my counselor observed that I seemed to be a person with a great deal of power and energy that I scattered to the winds with my erratic, undisciplined behavior. She asked me why I was afraid to have power. I replied that I had been taught by my religious upbringing that I should be humble, not call attention to myself, or ask for too much for myself. She looked at me and asked, "But what does humility really mean to *you*?"

To my surprise, my voice answered from an inner knowing: "Humility is taking one's rightful place in the Universe." My attempt to understand and live this inner truth has been a fascinating process ever since.

Humility has really gotten a bad rap. Generally, people think of humility as taking the "lowest" position in a situation. I have found that there are no real "high" or "low" positions in the world—there is only the right place for each individual within the organic Whole. Some people reject the idea of adopting humility as an attitude because they were erroneously trained in shame and self-deprecation in the name of humility. These people usually shift to a rebellious form of rigid pride and an inflated sense of self as a defense against the pain of this false understanding. I have seen other people choose permanent identification with the poor in the name of humility. Some of these folks feel righteous in their sense of separation from the rich and powerful. They may actually be practicing self-denial as a form of arrogance as intense as the wealthy people they presume are snobs! Humility is neither high nor low, rich nor poor. It is taking your rightful place *now* and serving the good of the Whole from that place.

A friend of Martin Luther King Jr. once described the constant struggle King felt about his position in the civil rights movement. He often felt that he was inadequate for the job, and that he lacked some of the skills and qualities he perceived were necessary for this leadership. And yet this "place" was continually offered to him by the mysterious force of this powerful movement. It was his place alone. How fortunate for our whole nation that he had the humility to continue to accept this position, despite his nagging insecurity.

Everyone is gifted in some regard. It seems that our life situations consistently ask us to serve the good of the Whole with our gifts, which come out of our characters and our natures. Our gifts contribute to the balance and health of human society. I know someone who has an uncanny knack for enhancing the physical comfort of any environment he stays in for more than a day. He serves the comfort of those around him with grace and ease; it comes out of who he is. Someone else I know has an intuitive radar for errors and missing details, and he has been an invaluable worker in warehouses and mail-order businesses, where these skills really count. Some people are natural counselors. Their good listening skills and easy empathy attract upset or needy people at any party or bus stop. Sometimes we find ourselves asking, "Why am I always the one who . . . ?" Well, because you are. You're the one who volunteered to clean up after the potluck *again*? Good! Do it. Humility asks you to give what you can, within practical limits.

I have known some bright, talented people who hid their light under a bushel because they were afraid to shine. They doubted their own motives and their right to take up space. They served a false notion of humility. Every time God offered them an opportunity to shine, they backed off. They sabotaged their own efforts so they wouldn't make too big an impact on anything.

If life is asking you to shine, it is a form of arrogance to refuse. That arrogance also lacks perspective. You are not the best or the worst who has ever come along; you are just uniquely you. It's your turn to grow and blossom under the sun, spread your seeds, and die. What if prairie flowers refused to bloom because they were afraid of not being the best thing on the prairie, or that no one would really appreciate their efforts? Humility is taking one's rightful place in the Universe.

I learned a new definition of humility from my mentor, Dr. Edith Stauffer, author of *Unconditional*

Love and Forgiveness. She taught me that humility is an attitude of perceiving another's needs as he or she sees them, and having the desire to serve those needs, if doing so is practical. That'll keep you busy on your spiritual path for a while: another's needs, as *that person* understands them. It is so much easier to think that we know what other people need, what their priorities should be. Other people may be telling us very clearly what they need, in words or behavior, but if we don't have an attitude of humility, we can miss the point entirely. We're busy trying to help them with needs we think they "should" have, and we get all lathered up about how ungrateful they are for our efforts!

Sometimes the practice of humility takes the form of accepting criticism. I used to have a tendency to feel crushed or very defensive if even a hint of criticism came in my direction. Yet many of the real turning points in my development have been triggered by facing an uncomfortable truth about myself when someone managed to get through to me. Someone once said, "Your faults are your obstacles, so you should be grateful to others for pointing them out to you."

At this point you may be saying to yourself, "Come on, what are you trying to do, be a *saint*?" Well, yes, I *do* want to be a saint. I have had the privilege of meeting a few souls in this world who have mastered being human—who are saintly. I have watched them in action, and it looks pretty good to me. I have observed that these people are first and foremost *themselves*, their personalities fully open, exalted like a summer rose.

I once took a heartfelt problem of mine to a saintly person, who was surrounded by hundreds of people at the time. But she acted as if there were no one else there except the two of us. Nothing was more important to her in that moment than serving my need, as I understood it. This moment of total, loving attention was like a healing balm for me.

In the company of a few souls on Earth, I realized that humility is a power as radiant as the sun. It is as strong as a thundering waterfall in its ability to transform others. Its power is an unimpeded expression of Spirit. I must regard my own efforts at humility with the same tenderness I would show toward a baby bird learning to fly. My relationship to a saint is like that of a baby bird to a grown bird. I must forgive my awkward flapping and falling. I must smile at the screeches I emit. I trust that one day I will fly in the clear sky of my liberated Spirit.

LOSS

See! I will not forget you—I have engraved you on the palm of my hand.

Isaiah 49:16

Loss is something we think of as an exception to normal life, an aberration. But this perspective must be wrong, because loss happens so often. I have had many losses: a child, a best friend, a family business. If this sort of loss isn't happening to me right now, it's happening to someone I know or someone on the news. No matter how much I say that life is unpredictable and beyond my control, it is still a major shock to me every time this proves to be true.

Every time I face a loss, I remember a few things. I remember that the Universe is simultaneously dispassionate and compassionate toward its members. It is dispassionate in that it is no respecter of persons. It does not *care* how much money you lost, how embarrassing your scandal is, how gross your accident was, or how young your children are when your spouse contracts a terrible illness. This cool dispassion is the meaning behind the esoteric slogan "Shit happens."

On the other hand, the Presence within this Universe is completely compassionate toward us when we suffer through anything, large or small. When I am reeling from sudden loss, I turn vulnerably toward that Presence, and I find myself in a warm pocket of peace and benevolence amid my grief. My heart opens in love and compassion for myself and others; I soften into the richness of the present moment. Every need I have is met, as fast as I can think of it. Friends and strangers alike become emissaries of this love. At these times I think, *I understand now. I will remember this.* This is the experience expressed by the bumper sticker "Love happens."

Then there is the problem of integrating my loss into daily life. This is difficult to accomplish gracefully.

After I have granted myself a certain amount of time to be emotional and get some support, I rally and get back into normal life. I have thoughts like *Come on, get on the ball, back in the saddle, back into production.* But it's hard to accept that I need to *be* with loss for as long as it takes me to heal. I become painfully aware that no one is paying me for all the hours I need to stare into space after a loss. I find myself resisting being soft and vulnerable to the Presence, the way I was in the midst of my crisis. There are times when I cannot bear to walk forward with the awareness of my real helplessness.

Yesterday morning, I looked out my window and found a hurt sparrow lying on its back out in the cold. I ran outside and scooped it gently into my hands. My intention was to move it to a quiet place away from my dog, so it could die undisturbed—its neck was obviously broken. As I carried it, the bird looked into my eyes with peaceful curiosity, apparently unafraid. It was still so alive! I didn't have the heart to put someone who was really looking at me on the hard ground to die.

So I brought him inside. As a child would, I put him in a shoebox with flannel rags and got him some water, which I fed him with an eyedropper. The adult, dispassionate part of me observed my futile behavior with wry acceptance. I knew the bird was going to die. But I had to care for him anyway.

The bird immediately fascinated my young daughter. Even though I warned her that we would try this only for a little while, and that the bird would probably die, she became passionately bonded with the bird within moments. She fed him water every half hour, cooed encouragement, and brought him pictures to look at while he was resting. She kept seeing signs that he was dramatically improving as a result of her faith and effort. I tried to reflect reality to her from time to time, but it was obvious that she couldn't accept it.

The sparrow died that evening. My daughter was stunned and hurt to find the bird still, his bright eyes closed. She threw herself into my arms and cried hot tears, still shaking her head in disbelief. She told me the precise details of her latest nursing efforts, and exactly how he looked when she found him dead. She gazed into space, absorbed by sorrow as we rocked together in the dim room.

This morning, she took his body out and looked at it. Again, her face wore a look of grave sorrow. She shook her head a little and sighed, still not quite believing that he was dead. She insisted that we take several photos of him before putting him back into his burial bag. Then we drew pictures for her to take to school—one of her feeding the living bird with an eyedropper, and one of her crying as she looked at him in death. She showed the pictures to her class-mates and told them the story. Tonight, I asked her how she felt about it. She said, "I'm still sad, but not as much. It's passing."

It seems to me that most of us are like children. We bond passionately with people and things with the cry of "Mine!" Then we experience grief when we discover that they really aren't ours. At these times, the Wise One within whispers, "I know this really hurts. This is just the way it is." We rock together in the dim light, pondering, staring into space. And healing comes.

CATASTROPHE

*The things planned before the world began come upon us suddenly, so
that in our blindness we say that they are chance. But God knows better.
Constantly and lovingly He brings all that happens to its best end.
When a soul holds on to God in trust—
this is the highest worship it can bring.*

Julian of Norwich

Catastrophe visits us regularly on a personal
and on a collective basis. Paradoxically, it is a
"normal" occurrence in life on Earth. Wars,
murders, abductions, invasions, epidemics, tsunamis,
and violent accidents happen in every place and in
every time. Peace and stability reign for a while in a
family or a culture, yet smaller catastrophes pepper
and pock those eras, too. Spills, collapses, small accidents, a black eye, a favorite toy broken—there is no
escaping catastrophe. It is part of the curriculum in

the school of Life. Besides the needs to eat, breathe, love, and be loved, the most common human need may be the need to treat one's own particular degree of post-traumatic stress disorder (PTSD).

Catastrophe is here to stay. It cracks us wide open to bring to us the kind of goodness that only catastrophe can bring. These days, most of us are aware that we dwell on the edge of the largest catastrophe in human history: the disruptive planetary transformation due to the impact of global warming on Earth's biosphere. As anxiety-producing as this situation is, I can't help but think good will come out of it. We will be challenged to the core of our collective being to learn how to live in harmony with the Earth, with the consciousness that we are one being, a fully awakened humanity.

I remember when a tornado hit South Minneapolis in the early 1980s. After the storm, my friend and I went driving around to see the uprooted trees and crashed-in roofs. Lots of other people were walking or driving around, doing the same thing. As we drove slowly around a street corner with the window open, I locked eyes with a man standing on the sidewalk. With childlike wonder, his smile dawned wide. He spoke his thought to me in a reverent voice: "It's a *catastrophe!*"

He was unconsciously delighted with how shocking this was. So were we. The sight of something large that is utterly demolished is peculiarly refreshing, though mixed with horror. At the same time, we yearn to reach out to people who are caught in the bull's-eye of catastrophe's hit. We want to help them, to serve them, and let them know that we care about what happened. Boundaries dissolve. Universal love and selfless service flow into the space the catastrophe created.

I have experienced a number of catastrophes in my life. When I used to think like a victim, I believed that I was dealt more than my fair share of dramatic personal events, but now I like to frame my experiences in a positive way. Clarissa Pinkola Estes, author of *Women Who Run With the Wolves*, suggests that you should count up your scars and wear them proudly as a member of the "Scar Clan"—the more, the better, for those of us who have big appetites for experience. The litany for me looks like this: as a child my house burned down, my appendix ruptured, my family had an alcoholic crisis, one of my parents nearly died, and

I was assaulted when I was a teenager. As an adult I became seriously ill for about three months, my husband's business went bankrupt, and he was injured, sick, and unemployed for two decades. I had three miscarriages (one of them life-threatening), our house was half destroyed by a flood, and someone close to me attempted suicide.

I suspect that each of us has a litany of personal catastrophes. They are electrified points on a timeline that is otherwise filled with "normal" life and lesser issues. When catastrophe visits us, it blows its hurricane winds through our stable lives and tender hearts. But like the man looking at the tornado's destruction, those terrible experiences become our favorite stories to tell later, our dark treasures. The spectrum of catastrophe experiences unites every person to every other person on this Earth.

One of the classic outcries after a catastrophic event is, "How could God let this happen to innocent people?" In a way, this statement shows our innocence clearly. God never promised to protect us from blind, amoral Nature. We are part of Nature, and what happens to us in Nature is *natural*. In our vulnerability, we desperately invoke God's protection from pain and death and catastrophic loss, but apparently He/She has no problem with these things. On the contrary, what if catastrophe is part of God's Universal Creative Toolbox?

In the Hindu tradition, God is seen as a trinity. There is God the Creator, God the Sustainer, and God the Destroyer. Brahma, Vishnu, and Shiva, also known as Kali. In this theological model, God spends time creating, sustaining, and destroying entire worlds and universes, just for the fun of it. For Westerners, appreciation of God's destructive aspect is perhaps an acquired taste. We are still attached to the notion that we are in control, and that we have dominion over the Earth with our sciences and our social order. We don't. Even though we Christians carry an image of an authoritative God barking out laws and orders, and a gentle Christ helping the lion and the lamb lie down together, I suspect that we are in a relationship with good old Kali whether we believe in her or not.

Kali, the Goddess of Destruction, is depicted as dancing wildly, wearing a necklace of skulls. Her fingernails drip blood. We are afraid of her, but we need her as surely as we need the pacific blessings of the Christ. She renews the Earth with prairie fires and volcanoes, and she doesn't sweat it if a few thousand human bodies happen to burn along with them. Kali knows that we are more than our finite bodies and personalities. In Hindu philosophy, we are the Self, eternally free from the limitations of birth and death. Particles of bodies, souls, and the elements endlessly recycle and reassemble in different forms in God's play of consciousness. Kali has no guilt and no regret as she whacks away with her sword in her whirling dance through the Universe. Good old Kali. She especially loves to destroy our ego and its illusions.

I've been forced to make friends with bloody Kali, and I learned to accept her as one of my teachers during a personal catastrophe I experienced: a life-threatening miscarriage that took place in the fifth month of a pregnancy. This moment with Kali is seared into my psyche and is one of my most treasured scars.

The onset of my loss and catastrophe was sudden and dramatic. I awoke suddenly from sleep at 5 AM with a gushing hemorrhage. I sprang from bed and sprinted down the hall to the bathroom, shouting for my husband as I ran. I sat on the toilet, cupping a perfect little fetus in my hands, and stared at it in wonder and surprise while my blood fell around him like a steady rain. My mouth was wide open and so was his. It was a tragicomic moment. I felt like the baby and I were looking at each other and saying, "Huh?!" That tiny open mouth reminded me of all the human "huh?!"s that ever were.

Though my heart was pounding with fear and surprise, a feeling of calm wonder and sweetness welled up within me. The room seemed very bright, clear, and special. My husband and I looked at the fetus and each other. When we realized that all three of us had our mouths agape in the same way, something broke open between us and we actually *laughed* into each other's eyes. It was a moment of a great transcendent love between us. It seemed like the bathroom walls dissolved like a thin veil to reveal a Universe all around me, filled with creation and destruction playing out on an unshakable foundation of unutterable love. I bowed a little bow to Kali's presence—I could almost hear her ankle bracelets jingling as she danced. We proceeded with the rest of the drama: shock, ambulance, hospital, home care, community support, grief, hospital bills, and getting up again. But I will always remember that sparkling moment of catastrophe in the bathroom.

The Hindus say that we live in the age of Kali, and I can believe it. Why else would so many of our block-buster movies be concerned with disaster? We *like* seeing the gorgeous, invincible *Titanic* succumb to the vagaries of human error and the ice-cold waves of the North Atlantic! Every night, of their own free will, millions of viewers settle down in their pajamas to hear the stories and view the images of violence, loss, struggle, and shocking events that our mass media pumps right into our living rooms. There is nothing that makes a better news day than catastro-phe; news teams roam the globe to find catastrophes if there are no local ones to report. The reporters doggedly run to ground zero to find the most pain. They pursue the people whose hearts are visibly breaking, or the ones whose hearts are wide open to their selfless heroism. The camera seeks them, finds them, and rivets our attention upon the very heart of that pain and selfless love. We watch, unable to tear ourselves away from the screen. We're in deep medi-tation on those images. Why? Because God is there. God is there.

GETTING UP AGAIN

After the final no there comes a yes
And on that yes the future world depends.
Wallace Stevens

There are times in your life when you feel like an actor in a play that has been rewritten without warning. There you are, performing your role as you have studied and rehearsed it. Suddenly, a flurry of stagehands removes the familiar props. Your leading partner is cut from the scene. You stare into the dim spaces outside of the footlights, seeking the face of the director, and feebly call, "Line?" Death, injury, divorce, disease, and business failure—who doesn't know the feeling of having the rug pulled out from under us, and hitting the hard ground of reality with a thud? We all go through these things at times, and we face the difficult task of getting up again.

The phoenix is an ancient symbol of rebirth, the spirit's triumphant renewal after apparent destruction. Originating in Egyptian mythology, the phoenix is a bird that consumes itself with fire every five hundred years and rises renewed from its own ashes. It would be nice if people could rise immediately from their wreckage in a flurry of wings and flying golden sparks, but the process is usually more gritty and mundane than that. It looks more like hobbling to your knees, pulling yourself up with some outside support, and leaning on something while you attempt to breathe evenly. Then, you limp slowly forward on a dimly lit trail, the horizon obscured by undergrowth. Eventually, your strength returns. Your trail meets a larger path and a clear view. Until then, you have to proceed with an ample supply of support, perspective, hope, and will.

When you are suffering from a personal loss or catastrophe, it helps to get some support from others who really understand your situation. You are not alone. Others are going through something similar right now. They may have more compassion and bigger ears for the details of your sorrow than your friends, who are tired of hearing about it. These days, there are support groups for just about everything you can think of.

There are also experts who can offer an experienced perspective on your recovery process. It helps to hear that you are dealing with something that many others have faced, and that your loss was not a personal attack for some imagined unworthiness. We need to be reminded that healing takes time. I have heard that it takes at least three years to grieve and integrate a divorce after a long marriage. When my friend fell off a roof and was paralyzed from the neck down, a rehabilitation therapist told him that it takes an average of five years to come to acceptance and happiness after such a change.

Recently I realized that faith is not a *feeling*, it is a *discipline*. Faith is a set of behaviors and attitudes you adopt to carry you forward as if your life matters, even though at a given moment you may feel that it doesn't. When you are facing a time of heavy emotions and lack of direction, it is an act of faith to tend to health habits like eating, sleeping, and keeping at least a minimum level of beauty and order in your appearance and environment. When sailors are kept ashore by stormy seas, they mend nets and clean the boat for future sailing. They know the storm is finite; work at sea will call them again.

It is natural to experience depression after a major loss. The discipline of faith prevents depression from getting too great a hold on you or settling in for a long time. Vitamins, exercise, fresh air, and sunlight will help your body endure this stress. Listening to music, especially stringed instruments, is a balm for a sore heart and jangled nerves. A good, hearty cry in someone's arms is certainly called for, too. You can discipline yourself to stop negative self-talk in your mind and switch your thoughts to positive statements instead. Though you may feel lacking in spiritual inspiration at the moment, you can build your physical strength and will until vision is kindled in your life again.

Your will is the spiritual mechanism by which you attain goals and manifest new dreams. If you lack dreams or goals, you can still go about the business of strengthening and toning your will until it has a new job to do. Establishing a routine and sticking to it is one way of strengthening your will. Rhythmic exercise, listening to drumming music, and accomplishing small, distasteful tasks will also help. I strengthen my will by insisting that I be punctual for appointments, since I am usually ten minutes late. Strengthening the will is the same as strengthening muscles on an exercise machine: focus on a number of small, isolated individual tasks in your life and work on each of them regularly. It may seem silly or futile some days, but strength of will builds, and eventually a zest for a new challenge does too. That zest attracts inspiration for new roles and goals in your life. At this point you can usually look back at your catastrophe and feel some appreciation for its occurrence. Sometimes you can even see how it was necessary for a previous attachment to be wrestled out of your hands.

History provides us with numerous examples of people getting up after having the wind knocked out of them. Wars and earthquakes have ripped their way through the human race time after time, leaving wounds and wreckage in their wake. Yet cities get rebuilt. People fall in love again. Poets sing the stories of heroes, and mothers cry their impassioned "Why?"

to caring witnesses. Going through loss and getting up again is an integral part of the human adventure.

A spaceship was sent out some years ago as an ambassador to unknown civilizations beyond our solar system. Inside the spaceship are artifacts of human culture, including a piece of music chosen to represent the human spirit. Out of the ten thousand songs that were proposed, the song that speeds toward our unknown fellows in the universe is a Bulgarian folk song—a message of mourning, strength, determination, and the thirst for freedom. It is wonderful that our scientists chose to be vulnerable to the unknown witnesses in the universe: to say, in effect, "Hi! We're here. It isn't easy. But we keep getting up again."

THE EXPERIENCE
OF FORGIVENESS

*Forgiveness: The profound experience of releasing an expectation
that has been causing one to suffer.*

*Unconditional Love: A refreshing Universal energy
that restores us to wholeness.*

The experience of forgiveness is profound and refreshing! Forgiveness changes us physically and emotionally, dissolving the stagnant weight of resentment and flooding our bodies with fresh new energy. It mends our tattered personal boundaries, and empowers us to move forward with more hope and creativity than when we were holding our grudges. When we do the thorough and gritty work that goes into releasing the trauma from the past, we reestablish our connection with our spiritual

Source, and that Source rewards us with a palpable sense of light and lightness. We find ourselves on new ground.

I think it's safe to say that there aren't too many people who actually *want* to forgive someone who's really hurt them, but we do want to feel better. It's kind of like having a toothache and recognizing the need for dental work. You don't *want* to go to the dentist and feel more pain for an hour, so you remain in denial for a while. But the pain persists, and you know that you'll feel better if you do something about it. So you muster the discipline to make that appointment, go through the experience, and get the job done. In the same way, we often put off naming the fact that we need to forgive someone, because then we have to *do* it!

Maybe we know we want to forgive someone but it seems hard and we don't know how. Maybe we are afraid that if we forgive someone who has hurt us, we will make ourselves too vulnerable and set ourselves up for further hurt. Perhaps we can't forgive because we feel that what was done is unjust, and we think that forgiveness implies that we condone injustice. (It doesn't.) Or it could be that we find so much satisfaction in feeling *right* in judging another, and we'd rather be right than be at peace. Usually, people are ready to forgive when they tire of the struggle and the story playing over and over in their heads. The need for peace finally outweighs the need to be right.

I once taught a short class which began with a woman defiantly raising her hand and declaring, "I just want you to know at the outset that I don't think it's even remotely possible to forgive my fiancé and my best friend for having an affair with each other three weeks before our wedding." She received nods of support from the other class members as she explained that she'd already broken ties with both of them but she felt like a basket case and didn't know how to go on. She didn't want to forgive them, but she couldn't eat, sleep, or function at work, and she didn't know what else to do. I encouraged her to go along with the workshop exercises that she was willing to go along with, and we then heartily engaged the whys and wherefores of forgiveness for a few hours.

After we had all practiced getting in touch with our Higher Power through a number of simple exercises, she raised her hand again and said, "I want you to know that I think there is a *tiny shred of possibility* that I can forgive them and move on." "Good!" I congratulated her. "All you need is a tiny shred of faith and a tiny bit of willingness. Then when you do the steps of forgiveness, you will find the healing you're looking for." And because she had already cried and raged her fill, and she was so ready to feel better, she forgave both of them and herself completely in a total of two hours' private work, and found permanent relief from this hurt.

Permanent relief? I hear you say. Can we really get permanent healing from the pain of our biggest wounds? We can. Forgiveness is a natural and transformational process—like fire that burns wood to ashes. If you burn a log to ash, you don't wake up the next day and find a whole log again. It's been changed. In the same way, if you work through an injury in all the ways that your whole being requires, as in The 8 Steps of Forgiveness—you are changed. Your own body tells you that this is true. I once forgave my husband's business for stressing us out for years and then going belly up anyway. As I completed the last step of forgiveness, I literally felt something go *"sproing!"* and pop off my chest, leaving my heart feeling light and free. I didn't know that I was carrying my pain about that business as a burden on my heart until I felt it leave me.

Sometimes we hold on to our resentment toward someone whom we love because we feel that the resentment is the only bond we have with them. A woman at one of my workshops hesitated just as she was about to forgive her dad for being incestuous with her as a child. Even though there was nothing more to say or do with the horror of it after seven years of therapy, she just couldn't let it go. She thought she would feel like an orphan with no father at all if she forgave him and stopped holding her grudge against him—it was her bond with him. I encouraged her to turn her heart toward her Higher Power as a Father, and let her fallible earthly dad off the hook at last. When she did this, and she completely released all of her expectations of her dad, she became flooded with buried memories of a good connection with him. She found her peace. In addition to healing her relationship with her dad, this woman reported to me later, "It's like all my senses woke up that day. I was numb before. Now I smell flowers and hear birds and feel the breezes as I do my work as a postal carrier. I came alive again that day."

This works for forgiving moms, too—if we turn to God the Mother and release all our disappointed expectations of our human mothers, we find a Divine Source pouring in the nurturing we crave. Nobody has to remain an orphan in this world!

From time to time I am blessed to witness that people can forgive the unforgivable. Some time ago I taught an *Unconditional Love and Forgiveness* workshop at a retreat center in central Wisconsin. On the first evening, a woman I will call Liz shyly revealed that she sought healing from the trauma of having been raped by her minister a number of years earlier. Her face was strained and gray, and her posture was tight and protected—the personal hell that she lived in was visible to all of us. The compassion in the room from the other sixty participants was full and warm as she spoke, and I knew that I was meant to work with her that weekend.

Over the course of the next two days, I watched Liz gather her will—the first step toward forgiveness—and seek through prayer and community to find the strength to completely forgive this man for his terrible act. She wanted to free herself of any further entanglement with him or with that moment. On the last day of the workshop I helped her descend fully into the hate and poison left within her from this experience, and in the course of an hour, she forgave her rapist completely, step by step. Sixty people sat patiently through her foul language and her vivid imaginary castration of her assailant. Releasing your emotional truth is the second step of forgiveness. As we moved on through the third and fourth steps I found myself wondering, "Will this really work? Can even *this* be forgiven?" Her powerful work pushed on the edges of my own capacity to forgive, and my own faith in the process. However, we both persisted in the process and—faithful as the sun—the light of forgiveness dawned.

As Liz approached the final two steps of forgiveness, and reached to her Spiritual Source for healing, the hair on my arms and head was standing up because the room was electric with Spirit's powerful restorative energies. It was clear to me that her nervous system was being flushed clean of the habitual patterns installed when she was victimized. Liz emerged from her hour-long journey looking as pink and open as a full-blown summer rose. There was a remarkable beauty and a healthy vulnerability in her face and body, and she declared with certainty that the trauma was all gone! Everything was silent for a few moments except for the soft weeping of a few of the witnesses, and then there was such an outburst of whooping and hugging and talking! I think that sixty other people simultaneously decided that they too had the courage to get to work forgiving people on their lists. If she could do *that*. . . .

If that wasn't enough to blow my mind, Liz told me later how it was that she came to be in my workshop at all. She was traveling across the country from Idaho to Massachusetts in her car, and at the eastern edge of Wisconsin she followed an impulse to stop in a church to pray. She prayed again to be healed of her hurt. As she left the church she noticed a stray flyer on a pew that advertised my workshop on the retreat center's calendar of events. An inner voice told her, "Go there!" *So, she backtracked two hundred miles to arrive at my workshop just as it was starting*, and got what she needed. When I heard this, it assured me once again that the Universe itself is conspiring to help us find wholeness, and forgiveness is a gift we all deserve to enjoy.

LIVING YOUR PURPOSE

*The Lord is inside you, and also inside me; you know the sprout is
hidden inside the seed . . . look around inside. The blue sky opens out
further and farther, the daily sense of failure goes away, the damage I
have done to myself fades, a million suns come forward with light,
when I sit firmly in that world.*

Kabir

"I am on a spiritual journey. I am seeking my purpose." Many times in recent years, I have enjoyed
the sparkle in the eye of someone who has discovered a hearty appetite for personal truth and living
purposefully. These people have a certain vitality,
focused yearning, and desire for insight and fulfillment
that brings the very air around them to life. Sometimes
there is also a sense of anxiety present. They may have
a feeling of having wasted time previous to this, or a
gnawing fear that time is passing too quickly and will

run out before their purpose is discovered and ful-filled. I feel the urge to pat them soothingly and say, "Relax. It's okay. Don't make everything such a big deal—you're doing fine."

I also know people who are so relaxed and self-satisfied that they are, in effect, almost asleep. They have formed little grooves with their habits and their schedules. They have perfectly adapted themselves to the bumps and fissures in their relationships, and they do not stray much from the predictable patterns in their peer group or in their own conditioned minds. They live like pleasant zombies. It's hard to tell if anyone is home, some days. My hand twitches: I want to grab them by the elbow, shake it, and say, "Who are you?! Why don't you find out? What are you waiting for?"

Why does this bother me? Why do I notice when people are in a taut or a loose posture toward living their purpose? Maybe because they mirror my own faulty state of tension in my relationship to my pur-pose. Faulty? Could there be a right and a wrong about this? Not really. This is more a matter of aesthetic appreciation. You can live your life like a well-strung violin in the hands of a master, or like a slack, dusty old fiddle in your grandfather's attic. I prefer the first way—the way of self-mastery. Simply put, a human being who is fully living his or her purpose with relaxation and focus is a beautiful thing to see.

Spiritual maturity is often a state of being that can embrace one of life's paradoxes: For every truth you discern, there is an equal and opposite truth operating in another situation, or even in the same situation at another time. A great Truth is balanced between all of the lesser truths you can think of—a Truth that is not told in words. A mature mind that expresses itself peacefully from the center of this Truth, while maintaining a full awareness of paradox, is as precious as a full-blown rose, blessing its surroundings with its pure essence. This intrinsic beauty is the "why" behind seeking one's purpose.

"Seeking purpose" is a paradoxical activity. It is both necessary and unnecessary to seek it. The key to discovering and fulfilling your purpose is to relax and love what you have. No, it's to get going and create what you truly want in life. No, it's to relax sometimes and get going at other times. No, it's to do both at the same time in different areas of your life. As the saying goes, "Nothing that you do really matters, but it's very important that you do it anyway." You see the challenge? There are paradoxical truths about seeking life's purpose that we need to understand and live by if we want our souls to sing well in the chorus of human expression.

So, you don't know what your purpose in this life is? Relax. You haven't missed the boat. Your purpose can't leave without you. You have time. In fact, unless you are out cold underneath the bed, with a bottle of vodka in your hands, there is a 95 percent chance that you are fulfilling your purpose beautifully. (Even if you are hiding under the bed, who knows: you may play a godlike role for the dust mites!) Maybe you haven't noticed yet what you are doing here. Give up your anxiety and relax into the effortless flow of expression that is simply *you*. Accept the true limits of your particular personality and don't try to be anyone else. Between the moment of your first breath and the moment of your death, there is plenty of time for you to fulfill your purpose.

On the other hand, what are you waiting for? Get going! Today is a good day to start. There are ways of being yourself that you desire but haven't dared to do yet. Don't waste this precious opportunity to be alive and experience things that you want to try. There's nothing stopping you but false limitations. You can use your will and your Higher Wisdom to discover and fulfill your purpose. Our world desperately needs your gifts and service, freely given. Don't hold back!

There are a number of levels to the subject of purpose. Everything from a mossy rock to a human being is fulfilling at least one level of purpose, due to the mere fact of its existence. I call this level *existential purpose*. You exist because you exist. If you add a few skills to that, and leave society in slightly better condition than when you arrived, you have a *social purpose*. This is about what job you have or what career or vocation you pursue. If you treat life as a classroom of learning, loving, and service, you have a *spiritual purpose*. If you pair up with other people to share complementary skills, you've got purpose in partnership, or *symbiotic purpose*. If you choose to call on more of your unused brain capacity and advance the whole thing farther along—yes!—you can consciously serve the collective *evolutionary purpose*. A single human being has the power to influence the evolution of our species.

The relaxing thing about looking at purpose this way is that you can do any amount of it that you choose. You can have a wonderful career, be a fairly decent person, and touch some lives in a pleasant way, but never once ponder a greater meaning than that. You can hang out and take the path of least resistance, but be someone's loyal son. You can embrace the new technologies of body/mind transformation and take yourself higher into the clear mountain air of higher consciousness, despite the fact that you work at the post office. You can be born with Down syndrome and live on government aid, but warm the hearts of people around you with your innocent and loving disposition. On this level, we are all doing just fine.

And yet, there is something in human nature that insists on asking *why*? We clamor for more. Something creative is hardwired into our genes. It bides its time until eventually it explodes outward in a surprising moment of genesis, initiating a period of divine restlessness and growth. Who knows what or who governs these cycles of rest and creativity? It's a mystery. I invite you to explore this mystery. Relax, and get going!

OUR COMMON
HUMAN PURPOSE

The purpose of life is to learn and to love.
Ralph

Anyone and everyone can live purposefully if they want to. It doesn't matter if you are very young or very old, schooled or unschooled, pretty or plain. It doesn't matter what your IQ is. You don't need start-up capital to get going. It doesn't even matter what kind of a mess you've made of your life—you can embrace your purpose today, and immediately begin to reap the reward of knowing you are living a worthy life. What is this purpose—our common human purpose? *I am here to learn and to love.* I learned this from my Aunt Ann.

My aunt Ann was a committed alcoholic all of her life. You could count on her to be drunk most of the time. She tried a few AA meetings once, but it never "took." She was well adjusted to her character defects, and much more interested in satisfying her curiosity about life and other people than doing any serious personal housecleaning. So, drunk she remained. Nevertheless, Aunt Ann never lacked company for long. She was warm, witty, and insightful, and despite the fact that she slurred her words, she was a great conversationalist.

My aunt lived in a high-rise on the North Side of Chicago, and received regular visits from her son John, his wife Meg, and their children, Brigid and George. She needed a little looking after because she drank away the use of her legs and used a wheelchair. John and Meg scolded my aunt in fear and exasperation when they came to visit and found her passed out on the bathroom floor in a puddle. She frequently sported lumps and bruises, and even a sprained arm, but nothing fazed her.

"God, Mom! I told you to use those handrails we put in. How long have you been on the floor?"

"Oh, jeez, Johnny—I don't know. Did you bring my whiskey? How's Brigid? Is she feeling better this week?"

My sister, Hannah, encouraged me to visit Aunt Ann when I came to town. Hannah, a writer, enjoyed plying Aunt Ann with questions about our family life in the 1920s and 1930s. Despite the astonishing amount of alcohol her brain cells were swimming in, Aunt Ann's memory and her present-time faculties were incredibly clear. Young Hannah always left from her visits feeling invigorated and nourished by stories.

"Go see her, Mare," said Hannah. "She's so much fun and she's as sharp as a tack."

I did. I waited patiently in the hall for Aunt Ann to unlock her door. I could hear her fumbling with the locks and swearing under her breath for several minutes. When the door finally swung open and I looked down at my tiny aunt in her wheelchair, I could see why it was hard for her to get the top chain off the door. It was high over her head. "Well, Mary Brigid!" she exclaimed in her familiar, gravelly voice. "It's so good to see you! Come in, come in."

My aunt tiptoed her way down her linoleum hallway ahead of me in her wheelchair, her little feet covered by absurd hospital slippers with pom-poms. She held her head high, and her shock of uncombed white hair radiated independent self-expression. Aunt Ann's cigarette smoke streamed delicately behind her like a banner in a parade. I felt like a visiting dignitary.

"Your mother tells me you married a great guy— Frank? Fred! And you've opened a business together. What do you sell?" She leaned forward, ready for all the news.

I gave Aunt Ann the full report. Her bright blue eyes absorbed every word with rapt attention. Her smoke ascended thoughtfully to the ceiling. As I talked, she asked me lots of questions, and occasionally declared, "Well, isn't that wonderful." I felt so good. The sunlight poured like a blessing through her high-rise windows. The half-empty bottle of whiskey on the table glowed like liquid amber. The scattered newspaper on the sofa could only hold good news. What was this feeling? My heart was warm and my person was safe as I talked with my old blue-veined sprite of an aunt. What was this? Oh, yes. This is what Love feels like.

One day, Aunt Ann's son Ralph came to officiate at one of our cousin's weddings. Ralph was a Catholic priest, and was enduring a long-term dilemma about whether to remain in the Church. He did a nice job of the service, as he always does; later, at the reception, he found himself sitting with a thoughtful Aunt Ann.

"Ralph," she said slowly, "What is the purpose of life?" Ralph didn't know until that moment that he knew the answer.

"Mom—the purpose of life is to learn and to love."

"To learn and to love. Yes . . . that must be it. I like that. Thanks, son."

"Sure, Mom."

The next Tuesday, Aunt Ann's daughter-in-law went to Aunt Ann's home for her regular visit. They always watched her soap opera together at noon. Meg was surprised to find the door unlocked. She was even more surprised to find Aunt Ann lying peacefully on the couch, neatly tucked under an afghan with her hands folded. She was wearing a fresh housedress. For once her hair was combed. The sun streamed in on her old face as the television chattered softly in the background. "Mom?" said Meg, softly touching her knee.

There was no answer. Aunt Ann was dead. She had died of natural causes about fifteen minutes before Meg's Tuesday visit. She somehow had the foresight to arrange to go with some dignity. At her funeral, we traded our favorite Aunt Ann stories, including the one about her last conversation with Ralph. We all came to the same conclusion that she apparently did. Our Aunt Ann had learned and loved, and her life and her death were blessed with purpose.

Listen to Mary have some fun telling the story of her Aunt Ann in "Our Common Human Purpose."

THE BIG BECAUSE

I stand secure, my doubts all dispelled; I will do thy bidding.
The Bhagavad Gita

"*Why?* I need to know why I have been spared so many times, while people who were leading better lives than I were not allowed to live?"

George's old face was troubled, and he struggled to keep his lip from trembling. As he talked, I could see memories passing through the screen of his mind like bad movies you wish you could forget. His fresh-faced buddies blown to bits in the nearby foxhole ... the car accident that killed a young mother while he only

got a scratch . . . his friends and colleagues succumb-
ing to strokes and cancer . . . All of these people were
charged with potential for success and a will to live,
but they left their lives in mid-sentence. Meanwhile
George himself struggled along fighting chronic
depression and inborn feelings of inadequacy. He
straggled listlessly through a long, patchy career in
which the only consistent note was mediocrity. The
worst thing George endured was the haunting and
accurate perception that even on his good days,
his personality was a burden on the people he loved
the most.

"*Why?* Why does God want me to live when I'm
just not good at it?"

I suppose I could have responded, "For God's sake,
man, you're just depressed! You need meds, *now!*" But
the wiser part of me saw that this was much deeper
than garden-variety depression. I saw that he was really
asking God this question, from his soul. He needed an
answer to this question, a fundamental truth to take
in as medicine for this long-term guilt and malaise.
And he was ready to hear the answer, so I knew that
together we would find it. For some reason that probably has to do with my purpose, people have been

discussing the meaning of life with me since I was young. On the playground in fifth grade, at the lunch table in the high school cafeteria, or in a quiet corner of a lively party as an adult—there have been so many times when a friend or stranger has pulled me aside with a searching look on their face, confident that if they spill their story to me the invisible light bulb perpetually hovering over my head will illuminate the answer to their question. This spiritual role became such a natural part of my existence that eventually I cultivated an intuitive process that allows me to seek and find guidance from Spirit for the times when others are unable to find it on their own. I did this now, with George.

Breathe . . . notice my body tension . . . breathe it away . . . notice my thoughts and opinions, my desire to "fix" his pain . . . breathe that away . . . empty myself . . . let go of outcome . . . fill myself with a desire to serve the Highest Good . . . pray sincerely to be of pure and loving service to this person, a worthy child of God . . . still my mind . . . quiet . . . quieter . . . like a lake with no ripples . . . Now I ask a single question into that stillness: *Why have You allowed George to live so long when it's been so hard?*

The answer came immediately, in a loud and firm inner Voice: "Because!"

"Because?" I questioned meekly. I had never known God to be rude before.

"Yes, *because*. Absolutely."

The answer poured forth from within me in a rush of comprehension that I shared aloud with George.

"Because. Because I said so, George. Sometimes you just have to live a life because you're here, that's all. A human life is like a day—so fleeting in time. There are good days and bad days, productive days, sick days, quiet days, hectic days—they all pass on their way. George, you're just having a bad day. It's passing. There will be another day. Your loved ones know this in their hearts and are willing to tolerate you while you're having a bad day. Basically, George, you just have to get through it, that's all. That's all I'm asking of you. Don't waste any more time worrying about it. Just get through it. It'll be over soon and then there will be a new day."

I opened my eyes and peeked at George. His face hung slack, very relaxed. He opened his eyes, which now looked tired and peaceful.

"Thank you," he said thickly. "That was very helpful. If all I really have to do in this life is get through it,

I'm very willing to do that. I'm glad that God understands that I'm just having a bad day. It's much better than believing I'm a bad person."

After George left, I mused on this for a while. *Because?* I always thought that each and every human life should be imbued with excellence and meaning, and something is going seriously wrong all of the time because a lot of lives aren't so noble. And yet apparently God isn't bothered about this at all. . . . Because . . . ?

A KEY EXPERIENCE

And in the end, the love you take is equal to the love you make.

The Beatles

"Oh, I hate this!" I cried in exasperation, as I slogged through the icy puddle looking for my keys.

"Come on, Mom. Let's go home now. I'm cold!" My daughter stood with her shoulders hunched against the wet March winds.

"But it's my full set of keys with my favorite key ring your daddy gave me for Christmas!" I wailed. I toed aside another chunk of floating ice to peer into the dark, sodden grass.

I straightened up and looked in despair at the sea of mud and melting snow that spread around me. Half an hour ago, it seemed wild and daring to prance and splash with my daughter and my dog among the great, old trees of our inner city park. Now that my keys lay somewhere in this muck, it seemed like the height of foolishness. The light was failing, so we walked dejectedly home. I imagined my car looking quizzically at me as we passed by, leaving it by the curb instead of getting in and driving away.

My keys! I missed their weight in my pocket. I thought of the lovely pewter key ring as my personal logo. It was a charming little open hand with a heart in its palm; it gave me a peaceful greeting every time I unlocked my door. It was well crafted and expensive, as far as key rings go. It would be embarrassing to ask Fred to buy me another one, especially since this was the third set of keys I had lost in recent memory. I suspected that this time my husband would reach the end of his rope with this unfortunate habit of mine, his sense of security undermined by the loose sets of keys at large in the inner city where we live. As I walked home with Tara and my disgracefully dirty dog, I had one foot firmly in shame, and the other foot in the awareness of an absolutely stunning red sunset.

"Where were you running?" Fred asked.

It was the next day, and the park looked like a different world from yesterday's wet spring evening. The light glinted broad and bright on the hard surface of choppy ice that covered the huge lawn under the trees. The temperature had dropped overnight and winter's unyielding face had returned. My little keys could be mired anywhere in this opaque mess.

"From there, to there, to way over there, and up there. It's pretty hopeless, really. I'm just going to report the loss at the park building in case they show up later in the spring."

"I'm going to keep looking," said Fred. "If children find them, they're likely to keep the key ring anyway because it's so cute."

I left him there and trudged to the park building, resigned to the loss. I searched for the day coordinator, dodging basketballs and shouting to be heard above the throb of rap music and loud voices of a small group of teens. It was the middle of the school day, but there are always a lot of kids at loose ends in my neighborhood, looking for a place to be that is not school or their less-than-stable family situations. The community center creates programs to serve the young lives that are flying about in chaos. I love the familiar whirl of vital energy here.

I found the coordinator, a friendly, besieged man with a thumb-sucking eight-year-old girl attached to his shirttails. He was moving what looked like a million folding chairs on a long cart from one place to another. The little girl trailed silently along with him on his duties. I didn't know him but I knew him: I had seen coordinators change here about every eighteen months for the last decade. Joe, Lenny, Sarah, Pat—what's this guy's name? John. They all seemed incredibly centered amid this mayhem, and had famously positive attitudes. They serve on society's front lines in the "War Against Complete Disintegration." I couldn't help the love that poured out of my eyes as I told him I'd lost my keys in the park.

"Lost yer keys? Well, I've got some fellows that don't got nothin' to do—they'll help you find yer keys!"

"Uh, no, that's okay. I could have lost them anywhere. If you could just take my number—"

"Pepe! Daniel! Mario! Come here, boys! We've got a job that needs doing! This lady's lost her keys."

"No, really, I don't think that we'll find them while the ice is frozen—"

"These guys are great lookers," he said, "If anyone can find your keys, I bet they can! I'll offer an award of one dollar to whoever sees them first!" His voice boomed with the positive attitude, but his eyes said, "*Lady, please! Help me out here.*"

I looked at the kids. They were all about nine. One of them was kicking the wall and making martial arts throws at the air. The other one had a wispy presence, and an unfocused stare that told me he wasn't quite convinced of his own existence.

Great lookers, indeed, I thought. The third child stood at earnest attention, staring up at me with liquid brown eyes as he waited for my answer. The combined intelligence of his face and the insecurity of his posture pushed me over the edge. I signed up for the "Key Project" instead of going home like I planned.

"Great, guys!" I said cheerfully. "I really appreciate it. Let's go."

We walked out toward the great frozen lawn. Fred was methodically combing the distant perimeter of the park. He waved at us and continued his search. The raw wind flowed against us like ice water, and the boys were chattering with cold by the time we arrived in the general vicinity of my keys. None of them wore a jacket.

"Man, it's f—ing cold!" said Pepe.

"Where's your jacket, Pepe?" I asked. "Is it at the park building?"

"Yeah—I mean, no. I don't know! Maybe I didn't wear one!" He attacked a tree with an awesome kung fu maneuver. Daniel stood vacantly nearby with his nose running. Mario clasped himself with his thin arms and said softly, "What do your keys look like?"

I described my keys to them. Pepe looked at me shrewdly. "Lady, is that little hand made out of real silver?" I told him that I thought it was pewter.

"Man, if that was real silver, I'd just keep them if I found them, and get some money for them."

He whirled off like a little dust devil out of season, looking here and there. Mario kept pace with me, looking carefully, his eyebrows making a line of concentration. Daniel continued to stand among the trees like a statue.

"I sure hope we find them," I said to Mario. "It had all of my important keys on them, and the key ring was a special gift from my husband."

"How much did that key ring cost, lady?" said a voice behind me. I was startled to find Pepe so close again. I told him about fifteen dollars.

"Then your husband should give us fifteen dollars if we find it instead of one dollar like the guy at the park."

I checked my irritation, remembering that I was now the director of the Key Project, and responsible for my words and actions.

"Well, you know, Pepe, that kind of hurts my feelings when you say that."

Mario looked at me curiously, and Pepe paused in mid-whirl to ask "Why? That's what it cost!"

"Sure," I said. "But I thought you were here so you could help me, not steal from me or expect a high fee. I'm upset about losing my keys—I need them. If you were upset about losing something special, I wouldn't take it from you if I found it. If I said I was going to help you, I really would."

"I'll look over here" Pepe gave Daniel a little shove as he ran off.

Mario and I continued our methodical side-by-side search until it was too cold for me, even in my warm jacket. We called in the troops. Between the five of us, if you count Daniel, we had searched every inch of the expansive lawn.

"Thank you, boys. We gave a good try."

"Maybe we need to dig under the ice," said Pepe, kicking the ground with his sneaker. He was finally making eye contact with me and trying to be helpful.

"I think we looked pretty thoroughly. I guess I'll just have to get along without them.

I shook Mario's hand, and he looked back at me shyly. Pepe slapped at my hand and resumed his attack on the enemies in the wind. Daniel was already gone, slouching silently back toward the park building.

"It was nice to meet you, Mario. Thanks for looking so carefully."

He nodded shyly, and turned to go. My keys were on the ground in front of his feet. Impossibly, the shiny little hand greeted him with its open heart.

"I found them!" he cried joyfully, pouncing on the keys and waving them over his head.

"MARIO! MARIO! MARIO FOUND MY KEYS! HOORAY!" Hopping up and down, I shouted the good news to the bitter, white sky.

"Here you go," he said proudly. His eyes sparkled with the self-esteem of one who has saved the day.

He was a hero. He ran off, catching up with Pepe and Daniel, and the three of them ran back to the park building to report to John. Victory united them. Fred and I made our way home, my keys resting heavily in my pocket. I was glad that I had lost them so Mario could find them.

"Honey," I said, "We do not know what purposes we serve."

WE LIVE WITH CROWS

One brings Sorrow, Two brings Joy
Three a Girl, and Four a Boy
Five bring Want, and Six bring Gold
Seven bring secrets never told
Eight bring wishing, Nine bring kissing
Ten, the love my own heart's missing!
English nursery rhyme

I live with crows. Do you? In recent years they have flapped their way into my consciousness, and now they are with me, day by day, throughout the long Minnesota winter. While I shuffle around in a sleepy morning stupor, I hear their raucous cries all around my house. As I put the teakettle on, they seem to shout, *Get up! Get up! It's a winter day! Quick, come see it—it's the only day like this, ever! This is your opportunity!* Crows are the bird world's experts in opportunity, and one of the reasons they thrive in our urban and suburban areas is that they are "human com-mensals," creatures that can use all sorts of human refuse to their advantage. They share a lifestyle with us, appre-ciating a landscape that has a combination of open spaces and scattered trees. In many places in the United States there are now thousands of crows—healthy, highly successful crows that have been replicating with gusto, season after season. I frequently find myself won-dering about them, especially in winter.

Crows are curious, and like us, they are commu-nicators and storytellers that pass information down to the next generation. They tell each other about resources and incidents, and teach their young how to stay safe. Scientists have learned that crows have good facial recognition and excellent memory for the friendly or hostile actions of people or animals they have had interactions with. They remember our deeds—good and bad—for a long time. So, it's quite possible that the crows in nearby trees are wondering about me too. As I hustle out to my car each day, my keys jingling, I hear a familiar cry from the lookout crow on a high branch at the edge of my yard. His job is to alert other crows about the appearances and disappearances of other creatures in their territory.

He utters a single *caw!* just as I reach the same spot in the middle of my front sidewalk—a routine announcement to his family. Sometimes I fancy that I can understand what a crow is saying. I imagine the lookout crow saying, *Hey, there's that woman who likes us.* When I first got my (cute, weird, anxious) little terrier and let her out in the backyard, a whole gang of crows overhead began to shout and guffaw. In that split second before common sense intervened, I understood with certainty that they were laughing and joke-threatening that they planned to eat my silly dog for lunch. I stopped mid-step and put my hands on my hips to yell up at them, "Don't you even think about eating my dog!"

Crows are like humans in various ways. They are *smart*, with complex brains that are capable of creative problem-solving; for instance, they can adapt and use a small stick like a tool when they need one. They search for and work to impress a mate, with whom they forge a close monogamous relationship for life. They are loyal to their friends, playing with each other and sitting close to someone special for a good conversation. Each successive generation of crows builds a nest near to the tree of their birth, and the grandparents babysit for the nestlings while the young adults go out to work. Older siblings babysit for the young ones too. Crow families live close to each other, steadily expanding as a clan, and they remain together for many years. The average crow lives to be twenty.

Crows are social animals with their own rules, and as some people do, they appear to believe in the death penalty for grievous offenses. The expression "a murder of crows" most likely refers to the fact that for reasons mysterious to us, a community of crows will occasionally cast one out, turn on it as one, and kill it with cold, purposeful fury. As social animals, they also seem to feel social pain, and they will grieve a fallen community member—crying, screaming, and wailing out a wild song of genuine loss. They participate in what amounts to a funeral for the deceased, with hundreds of crows gathering in respectful silence in the trees that surrounds a friend's dead body lying on the ground. One observer has witnessed a crow community conducting a sort of simple funeral rite: one by one, a whole line of birds hopped solemnly forward to approach the still body, "speak" a few words, and bob respectfully. Some of them brought small sticks that they placed on the ground near it, as if leaving gifts of appreciation or remembrance. Wonderful creatures!

The crow is preeminently the bird of Mystery. Around the world, folktales are laden with lore about the crow, and in some traditions they are seen as the heralds of death or ominous events. In ancient Ireland the crow was the representative of the Morrigan ("great queen"), a goddess of war, and brought omens to the battlefield about who would prevail. In later times, the countryfolk of Ireland simply thought of these birds as "lucky" to have around. To me, the crow's unmistakable, enigmatic silhouette will forever be associated with the best of what I believe about life's simple and abounding magic. Midnight black, bold and audacious, the crows near me are both obvious and inscrutable at the same time.

I've been lucky enough to be personally blessed with an incident of crow magic. About ten years ago, in the deep wintertime, my husband and I were startled by a loud racket of bird cries outside—hundreds of crows were crying strangely and flapping restlessly all around our house, and they kept it up for quite a while. Sometime later, as I went out my front door, I was astonished to see a large crow sitting on the tree branch at eye level, right next to my doorstep. He sat still and silent, his feet firmly gripping a small branch, his head softly resting on his breast. It looked like he had just closed his eyes in sleep, a sentinel in peacetime who had nodded off for a moment, but he was dead. Unblemished and beautiful, his glossy black feathers called out for me to gently stroke them, so I did. He was starting to grow stiff, and as I tried to coax his toes off the branch so I could put him to rest somewhere, I found that I couldn't budge him. His feet were frozen firmly to the branch, so I couldn't pry him loose without damaging his perfect form. *Oh, well*, I thought. *It's well below zero. I guess he can just perch right here until it's warm enough to get him loose.* It didn't warm up for weeks, so I had the odd experience of passing in and out of my front door a few times a day, and nodding respectfully at the sleeping crow, who remained ever beautiful in the deep freeze. Being superstitious in a cheerful sort of way, I assumed that this was some kind of a strange blessing or a message whose meaning I had yet to discern.

As winter turned toward spring, I made my first of many trips to Ireland, home of my forebears. I arrived by bus in Abbeyfeale, Limerick, where my grandfather was born, and my cousin Mary came to the bus stop to pick me up in her car. A few years older than me, Mary is both a farmer and a schoolteacher—a busy woman with a brisk, no-nonsense manner. As she welcomed me and took me in with her shrewd gaze, she informed me what we would and would not be doing during this visit, because it was calfing time. She toted me around on some errands in town, spooling out a dizzying stream of family tree information—easily tracing the branches of my ancestral clan from their roots in Abbeyfeale into various cities in America, and casually pointing out the oak tree in the churchyard that was planted by my great-great-great grandfather.

When we pulled up to the farmhouse door, and I stepped onto the driveway, a loud racket of crow calls erupted from the trees overhead. Mary stopped short and looked up at the crows, and then at me; at the crows again, and at me again. "Hmmmph!" she said sharply, with an inscrutable look on her face. "The crows are making a fuss about you. They've not done this before. The old people used to say that the crows know the family they live near, and they note the comings and goings of people. They say that when a special guest comes to visit, the crows announce it to the family. Hmmmph!" Again, there was the shrewd unsmiling appraisal of my face . . . and then she shook herself suddenly as if to regain some sense, and hustled inside with her shopping bags crackling. That was the first and last time I ever heard her say anything that wasn't straight-on sensible. I paused for a moment before I went into the house, looking up at the large group of crows who were now silent, looking down at me. "Greetings," I said to them in a whisper, sending them pictures from my mind: *the many leagues of wild Atlantic ocean . . . the vast land on the other side . . . vibrant crow roosts up and down the Atlantic seaboard . . . the wide plains and shining cities in the Upper Midwest . . . the crow roost around my house . . . the peaceful dead crow sleeping in the tree next to my door.* "Greetings from your relatives in America."

Crow magic is available to everyone who lives near them, especially in the wintertime when they assemble in great numbers for their winter communal crow roost, a vital daily gathering of the crow clan. Look for them about an hour before sunset, when the clear winter light is just so. Especially if you're stuck in commuter traffic, seek them! Look up into the sky within the full radius of your sight, and before long, you'll see them, flying purposefully across great spaces from all directions, heading for a gathering at a specific location. Keep watching! They are coming and coming, a steady stream of dark shapes guided by some intuitive group agreement about the location of tonight's meeting—because it changes from day to day. If you need a little adventure, follow them to where they're going, and you will be treated to the awesome sight of hundreds of crows gathered on some city block that has a dozen neighboring trees. There they sit as thick as leaves in the bare branches against the pink sky, evoking the memory of summer's leafy fullness. For a while the crow meeting is raucous with conversation and storytelling, with individuals from different families crisscrossing between trees to meet and greet, and share news. Eventually it grows quieter, and you have the sense that each bird has found its favorite spot, and has settled in. As the sun lowers, thousands of crows sit together in nearby trees to share that threshold moment at the end of a winter's day, and for just a short while the whole group is still. It seems that crows, like people, enjoy sharing a moment of silence. Crow prayer? After a while, a wing flaps here and flutters there, someone caws softly, and they begin to fly off again in different directions, back to their home trees for the night.

Winter is long, and by the end of it, we humans can be discouraged, and thus require a little magic. This winter, look up! Just before sunset see the crows heading to their meeting, flying in streams, outrageous and free. Like us, they are part of a big, big family. They are not discouraged. They are not discouraged in the least. *Caw!*

PLANETARY RECOVERY

*The day will come when, after harnessing space, the winds, the tides,
and gravitation, we shall harness for God the energies of love.
And on that day, for the second time in the history of the world,
we shall have discovered fire.*

Pierre Teilhard de Chardin

It seems as though most people I meet these days are familiar with the Twelve Steps because they—or someone they know—are in recovery from something. There are groups for recovering alcoholics, overeaters, gamblers, incest survivors, adult children of abusive parents, codependency, sex and love addicts, compulsive spenders, and people who are powerless over their emotions. I'm sure the list is growing. New groups are germinating. "I'm from a dysfunctional family," people say. I have heard this statement so often in the past few years that I wonder whether it's a new norm. I wonder if people will start forming support groups for folks who have had serene childhoods so they too can belong.

I can understand this. The recovery movement is one of the best opportunities to present itself to human society in quite a while. The Twelve Step program offers us what human beings want most: a chance to begin a spiritual journey with the support of compassionate community, and a chance to establish a daily relationship with God on our own terms. The program offers structure and support so we can leave desperation and isolation behind as we conduct a thorough self-inquiry and personal housecleaning. It offers daily practices to create and deepen our serenity. It gives us the joyful duty of serving others who need our help, from the full cup of our own experience. Ultimately, the gifts of long-term, active participation in the program far outweigh our previous anguish.

In truth, we all come from a large dysfunctional family: the human race. At the global level, we are approaching the point of "hitting bottom." Our life here on Earth has become unmanageable. Our ecological problems are so huge, and our society so out of control, that humanity is at the classic decision point: self-destruction or recovery? As in many dysfunctional families, some people are playing the chief role in acting out this destruction, while others live in victimization or denial. People in recovery and spiritual growth movements are the vanguard of change in the system. Like the family member who begins recovery long before the alcoholic will admit the problem, we can only diligently work our program, speak our truth, witness the inevitable bottom as it comes, and hope for the best outcome.

Recovery and spiritual growth movements may be the evolutionary thrust that leads the human race out of the mess our mass ignorance and addictions have created. According to physicist and philosopher Brian Swimme, nature improves on her designs by experimenting with certain "fringe groups" in a species. A species goes along, maintaining a certain status quo. Somehow, a little group becomes isolated from the others. This group experiments, creating innovative food or social habits and eventually stumbling on a way that is more efficient and pro-survival. They teach these ways to their offspring. After a few generations, the new way is established, and the experiment becomes instinct. Mysteriously, the rest of the species also adopt the new way. They "resonate" with the transformation that has begun in one strand of the community, and evolutionary change takes place.

The recovery movement certainly began as a "fringe group." Chronic alcoholics, feeling desperation and social isolation, set the stage in the 1930s for the new experiment of Alcoholics Anonymous. Those first AA groups built their strength in relative isolation from the rest of society. For a long time, they were treated with suspicion and misunderstanding by the general public. But they had stumbled upon something that worked, something that was pro-survival. For the first time, alcoholics got better and began to function well in their lives. AA resolutely preserved the purity of its successful elements by adhering to strong principles. The resonance grew. Sunny and simple, AA groups spread with the inevitability and persistence of the common dandelion. Now millions of people around the world gather and grow together in AA groups, and *recovery* is a common word in today's vocabulary.

I am intrigued by the fast proliferation of addiction-specific clones of the original Twelve Step program. Why are so many people bottoming out on *something*? Why has life become unmanageable for so many people? Maybe the recovery movement is the prelude to something else. It is said that religion is "a finger pointing at the moon," but it is not the moon itself. I have a feeling that recovery is a finger pointing at something, too. There is something else. There is something underneath our species-wide spectrum of addictions that calls out for evolutionary change.

What is humanity bottoming out on? What are we recovering *toward*? Some say we are hitting bottom due to the destructive extremes of the patriarchal-warrior cult that overtook society several thousand years ago. This is the hierarchical, male-dominated model that holds power, competition, and control as its chief values. In this model, resources are scarce, and we need to fight somebody to get them so our tribe will be okay. Somebody's always up and somebody's always down; the world is rife with enemies to attack or defend ourselves from. Oppression and exclusion are just part of the game, and the players are always shifting positions.

Humans have steadily lost their connection with nature, as well as the wisdom of our feelings, our body, our soul. "Developed" societies are filled with people who feel lonely and spiritually malnourished. We turn to addictive substances to silence the internal howling that is trying to get our attention so we can face the truth of our situation. If we're very lucky, we bottom out early and get into recovery.

In the last part of the twentieth century, certain groups in our developed societies have been experimenting with a new paradigm. Spiritual seekers are adventurers exploring a new world. We are creating this world right now with small circles of people. Every little recovery group in a chilly church basement is one more vibrating cell resonating change. These groups are strong enough now that they have the interest and attention of popular culture.

Time has come full circle for us on Earth in the new millennium. We are looking for a "new world," but it is a world we have known before. According to Riane Eisler in *The Chalice & the Blade*, new archaeological evidence shows us that societies lived here for thousands of years in peace and wholeness before the bloody times of our recorded history. It is good for us to remember that we are not fundamentally warlike by virtue of being human. We can grow beyond the paradigm of violence and learn to live in relaxed, loving presence with ourselves, each other, the Earth, and our Creator.

TRANSFORMATION

*Will transformation. Oh be inspired for the flame in which a Thing
disappears and bursts into Something else; the spirit of re-creation
which masters this earthly form loves most the pivoting
point where you are no longer yourself.*

Rainer Maria Rilke

I've always believed in the possibility that a major
planetary transformation for the better will occur
in the course of my lifetime. That belief is being
sorely tested in this time of worldwide chaos. It appears
to me that the quality of human consciousness is at an
all-time low. Ignorance, denial, and addiction are still
reigning in my world. I am tempted to draw some negative conclusions about the results of all this, except for
three things:

1. The winds of truth are blowing strongly in my life and the lives of everyone I know.
2. I feel my own consciousness traveling to a new level.
3. My hopeless city block is undergoing a mysterious transformation. Believe me, if this block can do it, so can the rest of the planet!

After the Gulf War "ended" and most of the nation seemed to settle in to enjoy the "win" like the afterglow of the Super Bowl, I turned the television off. I haven't watched it since. Something became hard, clear, and focused inside me, and I entered a vigorous campaign to know, speak, and live the truth in my personal life. Oddly enough, it seems as though most of my friends became involved in a similar approach at the same time. One of them referred to our "program" as a "Promoting Reality" campaign. She has decided to calmly "promote reality" in all the daily situations she's in, no matter how thick the isolation or denial in the people around her. I wonder if the winds of truth blowing around here are circulating to other parts of the world. Wouldn't it be great if our world leaders and our media would choose "Promote Reality" as their slogan?

Meanwhile, something is happening to me too. After practicing regularly for years, my meditation is now noticeably different. My mind settles into silence almost effortlessly. I am now able to spend time with people I formerly detested and enjoy an attitude of love and respect for them, even though they haven't changed a bit! I am able to work with people in my new mode of calm, head-on truth, and as a result, we are all flowering. I am getting more serious about my complete, personal liberation, and God meets me with the same degree of earnestness.

One night, I dropped to my knees and prayed to be released from my stressful approach to daily life. That night, I had a dream in which I saw my mind as if it were a house. It was a house of torture! Each of the rooms represented a self-defeating thought or fear, all interconnected in a structure designed to give me no rest or peace. I woke up and realized that I need to acknowledge that I *deserve* to experience peace of mind. I do not need to torture myself. Now, every few nights, I have a long dream that explores one of these rooms in my mind, and I subconsciously work through many aspects of it. I wake up in a state of new quiet and understanding. My prayer is being answered, and I feel more trust because I see I am in expert hands!

I recognize the same forces at work on my city block. It is a mystery to me why I live here, except that I love my house and it's the place for me to be right now. I'd rather live in a quiet, aesthetic, prosperous, eco-village-on-beautiful-land with serene, responsible people. Instead, I moved to a block that is a vortex of crime, chaos, and generalized ugliness. The blocks near us are fine—it's just this one that seems like a hot spot in our neighborhood.

When we moved in, we soon learned that the two houses to the south of us were owned by people who sponsored parties and fights on a regular basis. Tenants of the fourplex across the street left piles of trash and stolen grocery carts in front of the building. The house on the other side of us was occupied by a single mother with seven kids who was too tired and overwhelmed to enforce curfew or civil behavior. Then there was the crack house down the block, where cars pulled up and honked at all hours.

After a number of sleepless nights that first summer, I bottomed out somewhere in mid-July. I cried and raged at God about my miserable fate and swore hatred and revenge upon my ignorant neighbors. In the middle of my hysteria, my Higher Self whispered to me that I was in a lesson about taking a stand. I come from an alcoholic family, and as a child I learned to adapt to inappropriate behavior passively rather than confront it intelligently. Now it was clear that I needed to take a stand about the quality of my environment. Nothing less than transformation would do.

I approached this challenge on several levels. On a practical level, I put energy into beautifying my property and picking up garbage whenever it appeared. I calmly and firmly informed my neighbors *every time* their noise kept me awake at night. On a political level, I got acquainted with my neighborhood organizations, alderman, and Community Crime Prevention. I wrote letters to landlords; I called the police. On a spiritual level, I prayed for the lady next door, the slumlord across the street, and for the block in general. I forgave everyone for our lifestyle differences and prayed that each of us would find his or her rightful place.

Once a week, I went up and down the block with a bag, picking up garbage. This was both a practical and a spiritual exercise. I felt conspicuous and foolish, angry that I was taking responsibility for the mess others had created. So I breathed deeply and thought about Mother Teresa picking up diseased bodies in Calcutta. She saw God in every one of those people. I quietly chanted prayers while I worked, and I pretended to see God in everything, too. I practiced a mind-set of loving neutrality as I picked up sticky junk-food wrappers, cigarette butts, and cans dripping beer. I breathed away judgment of the people who left them there.

After about a month of this, the garbage appeared less and less. The block began to stay clean for weeks at a time. Over the next six months, a number of changes occurred. The woman next door became friends with an energetic young man who had a lot of time and talent to help nurture and discipline her kids. The invisible slumlord sold his building to a responsible, accessible man who gave it a face-lift.

The people on the other side of me decided to sell, and a sweet, gentle woman who loves to garden moved in. The crack house down the street went into foreclosure and is being purchased by a man who is committed to the neighborhood. The city is planning on removing some of the most run-down houses to cut down on urban density. The change in the atmosphere on this block is palpable, and a number of neighbors have been commenting on it. "Getting better," they say.

I'm not really the one who is *doing* all of these things around here. But I see that all it takes is a committed minority to accelerate the rate of positive evolution in any given situation. The world situation teeters evenly between getting better and getting worse: more of us need to add our weight to the constructive side. Come on, friends! Join the movement to promote reality! The place to change the world is *here*, in *your* life, and the time is *now*. Add a little truth, a little grit, some politics, and some prayer. Focus it with your will and deliver it with love. We shall overcome.

SPIRITUAL COMMITMENT

This is total surrender: to be what God asks you to be.
To accept that you are in the street if God wants you to be in the street—
to accept that you are in the palace, if God wants you to be in the palace.
To give whatever He asks you to give whether you are in the street or in
the palace—and to give it with a big smile. This is the surrender to God.

Mother Teresa

I have been living in a whirlwind of growth for a long time. I feel like a cluster of amethyst that is partially embedded in sand and grit. Some craftsperson in the employment of the Divine is holding me carefully, blasting away with a high-pressure air tool at the grit covering my beauty. The grit is the fear, rigidity, and willfulness that obscures my radiance and the true shapes and contours of who I am. Some grit flakes off easily. Some of it is very stubborn and requires many applications of gentle solvent to gradually work it loose. I am afraid. I am afraid to sparkle fearlessly. But I know that I will because I am committed.

That's the trouble when you give yourself whole-heartedly to the evolution of your higher consciousness. Eventually it works! I have been on a vigorous spiritual journey for many years. I marched out of the clutches of addiction and codependency. I left struggle a few miles back. The road curves into lands of self-esteem and shining personal success. As I look up the road, I have the eerie sensation that the picture is turning from black and white into full color. Where's the fear? I'm afraid because I see no fear there! I want to sit down on the road where it still looks familiar and cuddle up to an addictive substance or two.

When I was a child, I stopped my playing in awe one day; I saw a black man on television speaking to a lot of people. His radiant face and awesome oration spoke of his dream for a world without hate or suffering. My hair stood up and rivers of tingles bathed me as tears streamed down my face. I realized that this man was working in service of the Truth. I wanted to do that, too. I understood then that the only thing that really mattered to me was to grow up to be wise and free and to help other people do so too. I am a spiritual worker. My prayer is to accept the possibility that I will reap the fruits of my labor. The time for it is at hand.

I have given myself to the cause of the evolution of human consciousness. I work on my own consciousness by being obedient to the healing directions coming from my Higher Self, and as I master each facet of it, people come to me for help. There are people ahead of me. They guide and inspire me to greater self-mastery, as I hope to guide and inspire others. It's not a hierarchy of being better than another person. It's more like the color spectrum of white light seen through a prism—a continuum of consciousness vibrating in different colors, yet all parts of one Being.

I want you to give yourself wholeheartedly to the evolution of human consciousness, too. Starting in your own life, today, make an athletic leap to the higher ground that is calling you. There is no more room, no more time for fear or withholding from truth and love in our world. Come out of fear and control. Submit to living your love and inner beauty in your daily engagements. All the help you could possibly need is right here, right now. Agree to shine in service of truth. Become committed.

A better world will not arise from the manipulation of existing political and economic forms. It will happen out of a shift in our consciousness as a whole. The relationship of form to consciousness is like the relationship of plants to soil. If you significantly alter the pH balance in the soil, old plants will die out and different ones will thrive. We are changing the pH balance of humanity's consciousness by composting our fears and planting seeds of love and selfless service. A new world is coming in a mysterious manner that we cannot predict or control. It may take many more years for this shift to be complete, but it's coming. All we can do is submit joyfully to our uncomfortable role as evolutionary mutations of our species.

I know of a fine spiritual teacher whose journey took him from a small village to a meditation path in the Himalayas. He was then led to do political work in India. He worked long and hard with the best minds and resources available to address the problems of hunger and poverty there. He concluded that his efforts would be ultimately ineffective until there was a large-scale change in human consciousness. He now teaches meditation and the *Course in Miracles* to twenty serious students, who then teach it to others.

Occasionally he goes into periods of retreat for extended meditation. He is a spiritual worker.

Mother Teresa is one of the most respected people of our time. This is noteworthy because her work did not look successful in terms of our popular culture's glamour-and-profit mind-set. Her mission gives its complete attention to the poorest of the poor at the hour of their death. We respect that because we unconsciously recognize that she served the evolution of consciousness, which we are part of. If one person on the other side of the Earth regains his memory of love and his own worth for the last two minutes of his life, something great has been accomplished for all of us. Mother Teresa is a spiritual worker.

Several years ago, three spiritual masters from different meditation traditions left their homelands to teach meditation on a large scale to seekers around the world. One of them, Baba Muktananda of India, said that the voice of his guru commanded him to do this and be part of a revolution of consciousness. When asked why this was happening now, he replied simply, "Sometimes, such a time comes." He was a spiritual worker.

This is not to say that meditation is the answer for everybody—it is not wise to jump superficially into a meditation practice. It requires commitment and is best undertaken after a certain amount of physical and emotional housecleaning. The higher ground is different for everyone. Maybe you can volunteer in a World Peace run or walk for AIDS or be a Big Brother or Big Sister. Maybe you need to grow in recovery, improve your diet, get into therapy, or make an honest commitment with another person. Every bit of your self-effort helps every one of us, too.

Our world today is like a lovely old house that is in serious disrepair. It has been neglected by tenants living in ignorance, without respect for themselves and others. On the continuum of consciousness, people in recovery are like individuals who have stopped participating in this neglect and destruction. Spiritual workers are like a sturdy work crew descending on the old house on a long Saturday to clean, repair damage, and restore it to its original glory—with some thoughtful modern improvements. Is this worth it? Will this really make a difference? Yes. Let's add some reinforcements and keep going. Will you be committed, too?

WAITING FOR A
RAFT TO APPEAR

All shall be well, and all shall be well,
and all manner of things shall be well.
Julian of Norwich

The three of them were sprawled sideways across the yellow raft, heads flung back and mouths wide open with howls of laughter. Squashed together like sardines, Savannah, James, and Zoe tipped and teetered giddily while they sought balance in a rubber raft made for two people. James's long legs disappeared into the water on one side of the boat, and his lengthy torso extended well over the rim of the other side, but the two shorter girls at his elbows were slouched down inside it, their bottoms grazing the stony shore through the thin rubber. Zoe's long black braids trailed into the water, floating like seaweed. The raft bobbed dangerously close to the shining surface. It was already starting to fill with river water. Savannah's face was red and wet with tears of laughter, but she tried to pull herself together for a moment to listen to me as I stood nervously on the shore, attempting to talk some sense into them.

"Umm, guys? This really might be kind of a bad idea. You might want to think about this. It's a long trip to be so crowded. Savannah? Where are the oars?"

"We—*ha ha ha*—don't have any. *Ha ha ha*—don't worry, Mary, I think it's going to be just *fine!*"

"You don't have *oars*? I thought you were kidding about that!"

The boat began to drift languidly away from the shore, coaxed by the current that ran strongly in the middle of the river. James and Zoe attempted to synchronize their wobbles as they bailed out the water in the bottom of the raft. They were about twenty feet from me. I could still put my foot down and say, *Absolutely not! I won't let you do this.* But they were seventeen, they knew everything, and they wanted an adventure. I was going to lose this argument: I wanted them to like me and think I was cool. I was seventeen once.

"Mary, it's okay," Savannah said, making more of an effort to assure me. "The river's not deep. The current will take us home. We really want to do this. We'll be fine."

"But, Savannah! I told your mom I was driving you two miles upriver. I think we came a lot further than that because we couldn't find the landing we thought was there. I have no idea how far up we came or how long this will take you. This will be much longer than two hours. You'd better reconsider this, since you don't have oars."

"*Ha ha ha!* Cut it out, James! Oops! Um, Mary, we don't have anything we have to do all day. It doesn't matter if it takes a lot of hours. It's what we want to do."

"You have no shirts!" I whined. "No hats! No sunscreen! No *oars*, for God's sake! I didn't *know* that!"

"We've got these," Zoe said. She sat up and earnestly feigned preparedness. She waved a plastic bag over her head. It had three peanut butter sandwiches in it. "And this!" she cried triumphantly, holding up a half-empty bottle of water.

"Great," I muttered sullenly. The raft drifted further out and slowly downstream.

"Savannah!" I shouted. "This is your last chance to change your mind! You might hate this after a while and you'll be stuck! Listen to your intuition right now, this minute, and tell me if you really feel you ought to do this!"

Silence.

"MARY—*IT WILL BE FINE!*" They drifted away.

Defeated, I walked dejectedly back to my car. My mind was going crazy, but truly speaking, the inside part of me felt comfortable. I, too, thought that it was probably fine. Foolish maybe, but not dangerous. Nevertheless, I practiced my conversation with Savannah's mother and my best friend, Lois, on my ride back home. *It was a little further than we said. I know it isn't the best situation, but I don't think they're in any real danger. My intuition and theirs was okay with it. Lois, they really wanted to do it.* My reasoning seemed to grow lamer by the mile as I watched the odometer tick off the actual distance we had driven through thickly wooded country to where I let them off at a landing. Oh, Lord. It was nine miles, not two.

"Nine miles, and no oars? No shoes, no shirts, no sunscreen? Mary, there's nothing between here and there but miles of brushy forest! What if they get tired of the river, and try to get out and walk home? They might get lost. And I don't even know James and Zoe's parents that well." Lois's usual calm demeanor deepened to graveness, and her voice was gently incredulous. She looked up at me from the county map we anxiously hovered over.

I looked at her miserably. I hadn't thought of that. I knew that Lois understood that I made important decisions by intuition, and we both appreciated a kid's need for adventure. We had raised our rowdy daughters together since they were tots, with a shared understanding about that sort of thing when it came to safety guidelines. But what *would* I say to the other parents, or the sheriff for that matter, about dumping three barefoot kids in bathing suits into the river nine miles upstream in a little raft with no supplies?

I vowed reparation. I called the park district to find out how fast the current in the St. Croix River runs; Lois and I calculated that the river would bring them to our landing in about six hours, if all went well. Since it could be dark by then, I also called the sheriff to ask him at what point it made sense to declare someone lost on the river. I went home and worried while I baked muffins and packed a generous picnic supper. I had assured Lois that I would wait with her for the kids at the landing all evening at the river, if that's what it took. She graciously accepted all my efforts at reparation.

A few hours before sunset, Lois and I headed for our rendezvous point, well supplied with food, books, flashlights, and conversation subjects. The light was clear and golden on the blue river as we made our way to a large boulder that sat in the shallows about ten feet from shore. The rock accommodated the two of us snugly, and we settled in for our vigil. Across the river, a fishing bird plunged into the water with a splash and flew off with something silver flashing in its beak. The river flowed around us, unperturbed by this event or any, at three miles an hour.

Lois and I talked a lot, then less and less. We worked through all the best and worst scenarios. They wouldn't drown because the river wasn't deep and they all knew how to swim. There were no rapids in the river's course between those two landings. They probably wouldn't be murdered by a psychopathic hunter or fisherman—that kind of thing only happened in bad movies. The biggest concern is that they would get bored or confused, and get off the river to come home on foot. That wouldn't be good. They were barefoot and wearing only wet bathing suits; the nights were cool enough in early September to cause concern about hypothermia. Lois and I would have to face the embarrassment of calling the sheriff and requesting a search party, and be in big trouble with the other parents. (Presumably, the other parents were more sensible than me and sure to be angry that I let them go on the river like that.) Of course, they'd be found. This was Wisconsin, for God's sake, not the Himalayas. We worried anyway.

The color of sky and river deepened. We strained our sights steadily ahead, seeking a glimpse of our watery wayfarers, but the river bent out of sight less than a mile away, so our further vision was thwarted. We heard news of them from a fisherman going by in a motorboat. "Oh, yes! I saw 'em!" he said. "They were having a great time, laughing every minute. No, that was quite a ways back. It'll be a while."

He motored off downstream, leaving us alone with each other and the river, peacefully flowing at exactly the same rate. Silence grew as the sun disappeared from the sky. Slowly, delicately, the chilly white mists emerged from both banks of the river, like forest spirits venturing forth for the night, seeking a rendezvous with each other across the water. It was a little scary and very lovely. Lois and I looked at our watches, and made an agreement about when the real panic could begin. The river didn't know what time it was. We cuddled beneath a rough wool blanket together, waiting.

We heard them long before we saw them. Howls of laughter drifted to us from the distance, the kids' unmistakable hilarity ricocheting around the soft corners of the river bend. How could they be laughing and conversing with each other so *loudly*? We could practically make out their words, even though we couldn't see them. We knew for a fact they were wedged right up close to each other's eardrums. How could they still be laughing after six hours on a crowded, ill-prepared river journey? It cracked us up. Lois and I laughed too, silently, so they wouldn't hear us, as we lay in wait for them. We laughed harder and harder until tears streamed down our faces, clinging to each other for balance so we wouldn't fall off our perch into the river. The river murmured against our rock, unknowing.

It took forever for the tiny black dot on the gray river-and-sky to grow large enough to look like a raft bursting with three teenagers in bathing suits. They kept getting caught on the edge near the grassy banks, too far from the current to make the kind of haste we felt was appropriate at this point. If they only had *oars*—oh, well. Lois and I kept our silence, blending into the rock in the dim light. We wanted to hear every silly word out of their mouths before they realized someone was listening. Eventually, they had a long, hushed discussion with each other about whether there really were figures on that rock or not. Then, with a hoot and a *hey!* they recognized the landing. When they finally discerned that it was us sitting on the rock and laughing at them, they were mortified.

Savannah, James, and Zoe floundered stiffly out of their cramped positions and into the cold, dark shallows. They reached the haven of the shore, dragging their yellow raft limply behind them. We hugged them and applied emergency muffins while we took inventory of their condition. They were cold, shoulders hunched up to their ears and teeth chattering. They were sunburned. They were hungry. They were triumphant, but very glad to be rescued. They *were* fine. That river current flowed in the very heart of me for days and days afterward.

ACKNOWLEDGMENTS

Thanks to all the good people at Beyond Words; they make beautiful books and they are so kind and respectful to their authors. Thanks to all the faithful friends of the first *Kitchen Mystic*. I hope you love this new version and buy four copies of it, too.

Thanks to all of my students for teaching me so much. Thanks to my Mighty Companions on my hero's journey—you know who you are. I couldn't have done this book or anything else without you close by. Thanks to the Hayes family and the Grieco family for seeing the good in me and in what I do, and especially to my parents, Joan and Bill Hayes, who created a home life that was based in unconditional love. Thanks to my glorious children and grandchildren for their enthusiastic, pure-hearted love. And thanks to my husband, Fred, for absolutely everything.

May the long time sun shine upon you
All love surround you
And the pure light within you
Guide your way on . . .

MARY HAYES GRIECO is a respected spiritual teacher based in Minneapolis, MN. She is the author of *Unconditional Forgiveness* and the director of the Midwest Institute for Forgiveness Training,where she teaches her eight-step method of forgiveness. She has trained therapists in the United States, Ireland, Germany, and Kuwait, and she was a featured speaker at the 2005 Nobel Peace Prize Forum. Mary was a faculty member of Hazelden's Renewal Center for sixteen years,and she also taught spirituality courses at the University of St. Thomas. Currently, she works as a forgiveness coach and spiritual mentor at the Well Healing Arts Center in Minneapolis.